CULTURE OF BUILDING
THE ARCHITECTURE OF JOHN McASLAN+PARTNERS

KENNETH POWELL

CULTURE OF BUILDING
THE ARCHITECTURE OF
JOHN MCASLAN+PARTNERS

MERRELL

CONTENTS

MODERNIST BUILDINGS

HISTORIC SITES

INDUSTRIAL STRUCTURES

PRIVATE COMMISSIONS

NEW INSTITUTIONS

URBAN INFRASTRUCTURE

FOREWORD
PETER DAVEY

Few architects have worked with as many masters as John McAslan. Frank Lloyd Wright, Charles Rennie Mackintosh, Erich Mendelsohn and Serge Chermayeff are perhaps the best-known designers of buildings with which McAslan has been concerned but, from the first, the practice (first Troughton McAslan, now John McAslan + Partners) has been involved with rescuing and reanimating fine existing architecture that has fallen on evil days. To the firm's work on masterpieces such as Wright's largest building complex, the Florida Southern College (p. 72); Mackintosh's last building, the house in Derngate, Northampton (p. 80); and Mendelsohn and Chermayeff's British masterpiece, the De La Warr Pavilion in Bexhill-on-Sea (p. 90) should be added transformations of unfashionable buildings, such as the Swiss Cottage Library by Basil Spence (p. 98), and ones with less memorable progenitors, such as the Roundhouse (a splendid former railway building by Robert Stephenson until now considered virtually unreusable – p. 64) and the Peter Jones store in Chelsea (a brilliant piece of 1930s townscape and a splendid example of the building type, but much in need of rationalization and improvement – p. 104).

In each case, McAslan's approach has been to respect the original building while welcoming the potential of new technology to improve performance and permanence. The Florida college is a case in point. Wright's concrete wall blocks were failing badly, partly because they were made using student labour during war-induced material restrictions. Many thought that everything would have to be pulled down, but McAslan showed that the buildings could be repaired

for much less than it would cost to demolish and rebuild them, at the same time allowing many more years of use. An extensive research programme was instituted to evolve new uses for the buildings and, crucially, to develop new blocks similar to the old ones in appearance but made much more durable through a radically new kind of mix. McAslan would not go as far as Wright, who claimed that his walls would last a thousand years, but he has demonstrated that the new blocks are a thousand times less permeable than the original ones.

The practice's work on existing buildings shows key characteristics that inform the whole output of the office: sympathy for context and history, full use of the latest technology, and exploratory boldness – a willingness to experiment both formally and in tectonic terms. As a result, the firm has a varied output. One may not yet be tempted to say, "Ah, that's a McAslan building", but the diversity of expression – which matches the very wide range of building types undertaken by the practice – does not mean that the work lacks coherence. On the contrary, each building is organized according to a specific set of disciplines, which are carried through the whole

The Holland Park studio, where John McAslan + Partners is based in London, is a volumetric top-lit space. It was used in the seminal 1960s film *Blow Up*, directed by Michelangelo Antonioni.

conception and execution with rigour and consistency. The disciplines are derived from context, programme and so on. Often, although they pervade a whole design, they are carefully played down. This is particularly the case when dealing with fine existing buildings, but their response to the old, while sympathetic, is never fawning. When engaged on the De La Warr Pavilion, John McAslan + Partners worked its way into seeing the world as Mendelsohn and Chermayeff did in the 1930s, yet they used new technology to complement the old.

The practice's disciplines for working with old buildings and for making entirely new ones are pervaded by a number of underlying sensibilities. The first is a very refreshing optimism, which McAslan picked up as a student and trainee in the United States. It seems almost inconceivable now, at a time when North American architecture is ever more dominated by the real-estate and construction industries, that in the 1970s (before the emergence of PoMo, the realtors' style) the United States still seemed to be a land of wonderful opportunity – especially for young architects from a Europe still largely dominated architecturally by sclerotic bureaucratic functionalism. From the wood-butchers of the western forests to the great universities of the east, almost everything and anything seemed possible. McAslan is one of the few European visitors who has uninhibitedly retained their transatlantic enthusiasms and energy of all those years ago. As the great variety and geographical range of his work shows, he believes that he can do anything, anywhere – and make a good job of it.

A second sensibility underlying the practice's work is a commitment to

pragmatism – particularly to the practical transforming powers of ever-developing technology. Edinburgh University, where McAslan studied (as did I years earlier) certainly banged its students through the rudiments of architecture and taught them how to make buildings, but the course was scarcely inspirational. McAslan's period in Richard Rogers's office infected him with a belief that while technology should never be an end in itself, properly challenged, used and understood, it can greatly enhance the quality of human life – and our relationship to the planet – by changing the nature of buildings and cities.

A third pervading sensibility is more formal. Louis Kahn was at the height of his late-flowering powers when McAslan became so entranced with the United States. Time and again, the influence of Kahn can be seen in the organization of McAslan's new work. The influence, however, is not so much that of Kahn's last and very monumental works (who but a fool would dare to derive from these?) but that of the Richards Research Laboratories and that building's immediate successors, with their highly articulated plans, clear differentiation between 'served' and 'servant' spaces, and constant concern for human scale. Exercises in such organization range from the large Max Mara headquarters buildings in Reggio Emilia, south of Milan (p. 116), to the little De La Salle School performing arts centre in Manchester (p. 172).

A fourth sensibility seems to be emerging within the firm, namely a concern for the nature of the public realm, for promenade and congregation. Bexhill, Peter Jones and Florida are reinterpretations of different types of social building, but in new work there is also a concern for public life. For instance, the Sure Start nursery at Mitcham (p. 176) has a glazed central common area. The Yapi Kredi Operations Centre (p. 124), which overlooks the Sea of Marmara near Istanbul, is organized by means of a grid of glazed internal streets that not only act as servant spaces but also have real social functions, with cafés and places for informal conversation such as are found in traditional Muslim cities. Circulation has achieved dignity and a sense of urbanity.

A grander and more open public building is the proposed new concourse for King's Cross Station in London (p. 184). The intention is to provide modern facilities for a major station, to link it with neighbouring St Pancras, and to free Lewis Cubitt's noble and early (1852) terminus from a mess of dingy modern additions. The proposed great glass volume to the west of Cubitt's building will undoubtedly be a major spatial and social focus, and help to transform what is at present a most run-down urban quarter, bringing it into conversation with the modern city.

King's Cross is the biggest and most dramatic of the new urban infrastructural projects. But it will certainly not be the last. If present developments in the practice's thinking are maintained, John McAslan + Partners will surely continue to invent with courage and an increasing concern for the ecological, social and human dimensions of architecture. Will McAslan be able to keep up the pace? The last time I met him in London, he had arrived from China in the morning and was going to India the next day (the latter for Easter, but he never seems to take holidays without including at least some work). It will be a sad day for architecture if he and the team have to cut down on rushing about the world and driving the work with such energy and conviction.

EXPLORING THE CULTURE OF BUILDING: AN EVOLVING PRACTICE

experienced architects and designers emerging in their own right, does not mean that John McAslan himself is any less involved in the office's projects. He remains an active designer. The range of talents in the office, however, has allowed the practice to expand in scale and extend its boundaries, a process that continues.

John McAslan celebrated his fiftieth birthday in 2004. At that age, Richard Rogers was building Lloyd's of London (his first major work in the UK), Frank Lloyd Wright still had another forty years of creative practice ahead of him, while Louis Kahn, an architect whom McAslan particularly admires, was at work on his first really significant building. McAslan went into independent practice, in fact, as long ago as 1984, forming the partnership of Troughton McAslan with Jamie Troughton (b. 1950) with whom he had worked during his three-year stint at Richard Rogers Partnership. Troughton had been the first to go it alone – McAslan was inspired by the confidence with which his colleague had launched into the uncertain waters of independent practice. The partnership enjoyed considerable success at a time when many new practices were emerging from the offices of Rogers and Norman Foster, but was dissolved in the mid-1990s. The separation was entirely amicable, though for a time McAslan was

Roots and Inspirations

John McAslan + Partners is a youthful practice in every sense of the word, though one that is a major presence in British architecture. It was founded as recently as 1996 with a team of under twenty people – a figure that has now quadrupled. The leading lights in the McAslan team are mostly aged under forty: young architects who have come to maturity working with John McAslan and contributing heavily to the emergence of a studio with a leading presence on the European architectural scene. For McAslan, shaping the practice with his team is part of a process of "opening it up", rewarding achievement and preparing the way for it to develop for the next quarter century or more. "I'd like to think that this is the beginning of a new chapter for the practice in which I'll be very much involved", he says. "My grandfather worked as a lawyer well into his eighties – work is in our blood." The process of shaping is now very much under way. The growth of the team, with a group of

which he remains greatly attached. Early
influences included not only Charles
Rennie Mackintosh – an architect who,
like Wright, has acquired the status of folk
hero – but also other products of Glasgow's
venerable architectural tradition such as
Alexander 'Greek' Thomson, James Salmon
and 'Tommy' Tait. Dunoon was originally
an affluent Edwardian suburb-cum-resort,
the sort of place where Glasgow merchants
once had mansions, commuting to the
city by steamer. These days, as McAslan
says with clear affection, "it's a fading,
time-warp sort of place". Dunoon was,
however, close enough to industrial
Clydeside for the local heritage of industry
to impress itself on the young architect.
The integrity and directness of the region's
industrial architecture still has an enormous
appeal for him, as does the directness and
humour of its people. "These are my roots,"
he says, "and for better or worse they've
helped shape my view of the world."

The west coast of Scotland has, for
centuries, had close relations with North
America; indeed, the scale and style of
Glasgow, with its dramatic history and
architectural consistency, sometimes seem
more American than British. The United
States has had a huge influence on
McAslan's personal and professional life.
His father, a doctor, took a post in the USA
while McAslan was still a boy, and the
architect was later to become a frequent
visitor to the country. Baltimore, where
McAslan senior worked (and where he
established one of the world's first trauma
units at the city's Johns Hopkins University
Hospital), was a city much like Glasgow, a

faced with the problem of having to run
a studio virtually single-handed. He is
the first to acknowledge Troughton's
major contribution to the success of
the partnership, and credits as "entirely
Jamie's" a number of Troughton McAslan's
buildings: the Jubilee Line Extension station
and bus terminus at Canning Town, for
example, or the office scheme on Rosebery
Avenue. In large part, however, the work of
Troughton McAslan and John McAslan +
Partners forms a seamless entity, with a
number of key personalities – Murray
Smith, Adam Brown, Aidan Potter and
Andrew Pryke, for instance – having spent
almost their entire career with McAslan.
This serves to reinforce the sense of
continuity in the office.

It is hard to think of a British practice
of similar size and vintage that has more
cosmopolitan connections than does John
McAslan + Partners: there are completed
buildings or ongoing projects in Japan,
the United States, Turkey, Italy and
Morocco. McAslan's roots are, however,
firmly Scottish. He was born in Glasgow
and spent his childhood in Dunoon in the
west of Scotland, a part of the world to

port and industrial hub. To the young
McAslan the United States seemed a
futuristic place of romance and magic,
a place where anything was possible. It
was an image fostered by the books and
magazines passed on by US servicemen
serving at the nearby Holy Loch base that
he so eagerly devoured. Indeed, from an
early age McAslan was intent on working
in the United States: while a student at
Edinburgh he spent summer vacations
working across the Atlantic (in Baltimore
and Boston) and he was also to spend
time there after graduating.

The School of Architecture at Edinburgh University, which he entered in 1972, gave McAslan a sound professional grounding but he found it a relatively insular place, with little contact with the wider world. A similar charge could be laid against the large Scottish practice in which McAslan spent his 'year out': "It was deadly dull," he recalls, "an excellent example of a practice that couldn't sustain itself without its founding partner." (Ironically, the practice was that of Sir Basil Spence, whose Swiss Cottage Library was later to be remodelled by John McAslan + Partners.) It exemplified the static culture of the typical British architectural firm at the time: "Architecture was never discussed at all", McAslan recalls. "It was a place of compartmented offices along corridors. We got together for silent coffee breaks in an airless basement room." It was in 1976, the year of the USA's bicentenary, that he was able to make an extended tour of that country. Here he saw buildings that he still regards as icons: Wright's Fallingwater, for example, and

Kahn's Art Gallery and Mellon Center for British Art at Yale University, New Haven, as well as the Richards Medical Research Laboratories in Philadelphia. He was inspired by the sheer variety of wonderful buildings that he saw, ranging from Corbusier's work at Harvard to the best of H.H. Richardson, Daniel Burnham and Louis Sullivan. Two years later, in 1978, McAslan was back in the United States, beginning a two-year term in the office of Cambridge Seven Associates in Cambridge, Massachusetts. By this time McAslan had met his wife, Dava, a native of Syracuse, NY, and a uniquely close US connection was forged.

The ethos of Cambridge Seven, "theoretical, artistic and strongly visual", was much to McAslan's taste and quite unlike anything he had found in a British practice. He recalls: "It was a multi-skilled studio and rather different from a big

single-head design factory, like those of Rogers or Foster. In a way, our practice is somewhere between the two." British architecture was, however, in a state of transition at that time. While McAslan was a student, Norman Foster had completed the extraordinary Willis Faber & Dumas headquarters in Ipswich, while Richard Rogers, with his then partner Renzo Piano, had been responsible for the most talked-about new building in Europe, the Centre Georges Pompidou. The Foster and Rogers offices were already nurseries of talent – indeed, many young architects seemed to move freely between one and the other. It was to the Rogers office, where people like Alan Stanton, Jan Kaplicky, David Chipperfield, Eva Jiricna and Chris Wilkinson launched their careers, that McAslan turned when he decided that the time had come to go back to the UK. (McAslan recalls: "I only intended to return to Britain temporarily, and always imagined I'd work and live in America. It was the Rogers office, and the excitement of living in London, that made me stay.") A friend, Judy Bing, introduced him to Rogers and his partner John Young when the two were on a visit to Boston, and the deal was done. McAslan was soon working in the Rogers studio at Princes Place in London's Holland Park, a former industrial building that had been economically but stylishly converted

by Young (Michelangelo Antonioni used it
as the setting for much of the film *Blow Up*)
and had the air as much of an academy
as of a workplace. It was refreshingly
unhierarchical and even a little chaotic; the
contrast with the Spence office in Edinburgh
was dramatic. To this day, McAslan regards
his time there as a highly formative
influence on his career: 'It really worked as
a studio, a place where ideas were shared
and views freely discussed. There was a
feeling that architecture mattered, both for
its own sake and for its impact on society."
The multi-disciplinary character of the office
was reinforced by the presence of the firm
PA Technology, which shared the space
with Rogers; the two teams occasionally
collaborated on projects. John McAslan's
almost obsessive concern for continuity is
reflected in the pleasure he now feels in
moving his own practice into Princes Place.
"It's all rather odd," he admits, "returning
again to occupy the same space where I
sat twenty years ago."

Rogers was then building Lloyd's of
London, and McAslan was inevitably drafted
in to help with the project for a time. Jamie
Troughton was a key member of the team.
"My role in Lloyd's was very minor", says
McAslan modestly. His own principal jobs
for Rogers were the two buildings designed
for PA Technology, one at Cambridge and
the other at Princeton in the USA. For the
Princeton building McAslan acted as project
architect, developing the scheme from initial
sketches right through to construction.
Richard Rogers has always rejected the

description of his work as 'High-tech' – the
term is now part of architectural history –
but the architecture that his office was
producing at this period, with its frank
celebration of servicing and Kahn-inspired
juxtaposition of 'served' and 'servant'
spaces, suggested that the term had some
validity. For a time, this approach was to
influence the work of Troughton McAslan.

The early work of the young partnership,
once Troughton had persuaded McAslan to

take the leap from Rogers and join him
as a partner, consisted of conversions of
existing buildings. This process had been
encouraged by the UK Government's
liberalization of the planning system, a
process that broke down the distinction
between industrial and office use. Former
factories and warehouses provided ideal
accommodation for the new 'creative'
(largely media-based) industries that were
starting to colonize formerly run-down
quarters of London. The first job that the
firm completed was a conversion of a 1950s
car showroom in Camden Town into Design
House. A number of similar schemes
followed, all of them economical but at the
same time imbued with a strong sense of
expression. They laid the ground for a
strand in McAslan's work – that of adaptive

Context and Continuity

Issues of context and continuity matter greatly to McAslan and this concern has infused the practice's work. He also has a strong sense of the relevance of history. With McAslan, though, history is something to be digested, comprehended and leavened with new thinking, rather than an excuse for pastiche. (The Princes Tower apartment block in Rotherhithe, of 1990, was perhaps the nearest thing to pastiche that the office produced – but in its time it was a refreshing antidote to Docklands Post-modernism.) At the core of McAslan's architecture is a determination to learn from history and to draw on its dynamic – in the design of new buildings as well as the repair and reuse of old ones. Though he launched his career with conversions of relatively ordinary old buildings, John McAslan has since tackled the repair and reuse of some quite extraordinary historic structures. He sees the practice's strength as lying less in repair than in updating buildings and equipping them for continued life, with the new interventions being clearly expressed. The De La Warr Pavilion at Bexhill-on-Sea, Grade I listed and acknowledged as one of the key Modern Movement monuments in Britain, is a case in point. It was an extraordinarily radical building in its time, both structurally and socially, and one that put Bexhill on the map. When McAslan became involved with the building in 1991

reuse, with an emphasis on realizing the potential of old buildings rather than rigidly preserving them unaltered – that remains extremely important today. At the Shepherd's Bush Studios (1985) in west London, boldly exposed service ducts in the Rogers mould were prominent internal features. The wall of glass bricks inserted into the later St Peter's Street Studios in Islington was a modest reflection of the influence of Pierre Chareau and Bernard Bijvoet's Maison de Verre in Paris, a building that Rogers had brought to McAslan's attention.

Troughton McAslan's first new-build project was the office and research building for Apple Computers at Stockley Park, west of London, the model for a generation of out-of-town business parks. The Apple building featured exuberant fabric sails shading a glazed façade and an internal 'street' that prefigured the Yapi Kredi Operations Centre. However, when it came to the design of a headquarters building for the Financial Services Authority at Canary Wharf in London's Docklands – Troughton

McAslan was the only British practice to win a commission in the first phase of development there – the influences were clearly of an earlier vintage. The smooth, curvaceous lines of 25 North Colonnade recalled the streamlined fashion of the 1930s and especially, perhaps, the work of Owen Williams, whose buildings for the *Daily Express* in London, Manchester and Glasgow were much admired by McAslan. Howe & Lescaze's Philadelphia Saving Fund Society Building in Philadelphia, and Wright's Johnson Wax Headquarters in Racine, Wisconsin, are other sources that suggest themselves. Today, the straight-forwardness of the Canary Wharf building retains its appeal (and has set the tone for more recent additions to the complex), while many of the other buildings in the first phase of development, decked in once-fashionable Post-modernist detail, look pretentious and dated.

it was in a dire state, physically deteriorating and in danger of closure or even demolition. After media coverage had highlighted the plight of the building, he came forward to advise the local voluntary trust that was campaigning for its restoration and was subsequently appointed by the local authority to draw up a repair strategy. With JMP director Adam Brown running the project, the practice has stuck with the pavilion through difficult times. As McAslan himself says: "With some projects there's no quick fix – you have to slog it out however long it takes." Funding for repair work was initially very limited, and was even scarcer when it came to making much-needed improvements – for example, to the public areas. The practice's advocacy was vital in terms of securing support from the local authority, English Heritage and the Heritage Lottery Fund. Gradually the most pressing

repairs to the external envelope were done, and the process of internal refurbishment began with a revamped café/bar, exhibition gallery and refurbished theatre. With some inspired management, the pavilion started to attract a wider audience and began to be seen as a regional, rather than purely local, arts facility. This recognition was the key to securing the substantial Lottery funds required to complete the remodelling of the building in 2005.

Although Adam Brown has been consistently involved in a number of John McAslan + Partners' historic building projects, there has never been, he says, any intention to establish a specialist team in the office confining itself to work of this kind. (As John McAslan emphasizes, working with old buildings is "a process of discovery and reinvention. We use the lessons of the past to inform our approach to new work, which we aim to make compelling, distinctive and clear.") Brown has been with McAslan since he left the School of Architecture at Edinburgh University in 1991. Along with Murray Smith, Andrew Pryke and Aidan Potter, he is now part of the team leading the practice, and is particularly involved in managing large projects such as King's Cross Station. The De La Warr Pavilion was his first job at Troughton McAslan, and he is seeing it through to completion despite the fact that he "came out of college desperate to design new buildings, not mend old ones". He stresses the fact that in every historic building project done by the practice, new design is inevitably involved alongside repair

and restoration. "Our starting point is: how can you change a building to make it work better and therefore give it a life for the future", he says.

While there are certainly a number of other British practices that have established a reputation for restoring Modern Movement masterpieces, the talent that John McAslan + Partners demonstrates in tackling large-scale schemes that involve both reuse and bold new interventions is one that is all too rare. The comprehensive reconstruction of London's Peter Jones department store is a prime example of this aspect of its work,

Curtain walls: Peter Jones
store and Erich Mendelsohn's
Schocken store, Chemnitz,
Germany

involving not only repairing the old but also making the process of renewal and change quite explicit. The store is a modern classic, designed by a youthful partnership in the mid-1930s and clearly inspired by the work of Erich Mendelsohn – in particular his Schocken department stores in Stuttgart and Chemnitz, which date from the late 1920s. Though clearly a product of the 'new architecture', the building was well liked from the start and is now listed. Indeed, in retail as much as architectural terms, it is an apparently immoveable London landmark. Not many years ago, however, the future of Peter Jones was extremely uncertain. The outbreak of the Second World War had halted construction

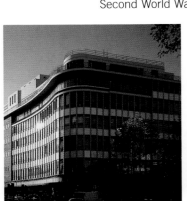 

midway – it did not begin again in earnest until after 1960 – and while the great curtain wall wrapping around the corner of the King's Road was complete, the interior was far from finished. Parts of the former (Victorian) store to the rear remained, though they had been earmarked for clearance, and they are now likely to remain in perpetuity. The post-war completion of the building involved many compromises. The phased construction of the store was reflected in an apparently random skyline and, inside the building, by badly connected spaces with inconvenient changes of floor level. Services were, by late twentieth-century standards, very inadequate and were overdue for replacement. When the John Lewis Partnership approached Kensington & Chelsea Council to discuss a major reconstruction, however, its proposals for additional floors and rooftop extensions for new servicing were firmly rejected. The company faced the dilemma of running a historic building that, though well loved, was increasingly obsolete as a modern retail facility.

It was obvious from the start of John McAslan + Partners' involvement with Peter Jones that this was another project where a 'quick fix' was out of the question. It was inconceivable that the store could close completely, even for a short period. The decision was made to reconstruct it in phases over five years, with departments reorganized within the building or temporarily decanted to another building ('PJ2') about 800 metres (half a mile) away. The McAslan team devised the phasing strategy for the scheme, which has been implemented in three stages, with two of the three phased elements in the project remaining in use throughout the construction operation. Correctly, as it turned out, the management believed that its loyal customers would tolerate a degree of inconvenience in the short term in order

to re-equip Peter Jones for a new century. Certain elements in the project – new services and a rationalization of floor levels and internal connections, for example – were fundamental, though extended negotiations with local planners, English Heritage and the Twentieth Century Society were needed to secure the necessary consents. Where the project moved beyond the realm of reinstatement and restoration was in its transformation of the listed building. The creation of a new, full-height central atrium, with all floors linked by escalators, was a very bold move, giving Peter Jones a space to compare, for example, with the great stores of Paris (or, for that matter, with the atrium at Lloyd's). In a heritage-fixated culture, where concern for detail sometimes counts for more than a vision for the whole, the realization of this project is quite an achievement, but it exemplifies the willingness of the McAslan office to challenge preconceptions about the 'correct' way of dealing with old buildings.

McAslan has long argued that the US concept of 'adaptive reuse' deserves to be more widely studied and understood in the UK, where the philosophy of historic buildings' repair and reuse sometimes seems to be stuck in the age of Ruskin and Morris. In the United States, federal guidelines define rehabilitation as "the process of returning a property to a state of utility, through repair or alteration, which late 1930s and late 1950s, dismayed McAslan. The 'textile blocks' that Wright used in their construction had weathered badly; some had crumbled, exposing the steel reinforcement bars underneath, and the range of techniques used in attempts to repair them seemed to have failed. Moreover, several buildings were suffering from the dramatic failure of flat roofs. McAslan sought a meeting with college president Dr Robert Davis, who confirmed that many years of costly repair works appeared to have done little good and that the Wright buildings were widely seen as a heavy burden for the college rather than as an asset.

McAslan had to help raise the funding that was needed to kick-start the process of restoration. More than a decade on, John McAslan + Partners has put together a masterplan for the future development of the campus, completed new student residences and carried out a comprehensive $10 million remodelling of the largest of the Wright buildings, the 1950s Polk County Science Center, which had faced closure on account of its rotting fabric and deteriorating services. The internal spaces have been radically reconfigured in line with modern requirements and new

makes possible an efficient contemporary use, while preserving those portions and features of the property which are significant to its historic, architectural and cultural value." These guidelines were highly relevant, of course, to John McAslan + Partners' work at Florida Southern College, located near Tampa.

Florida Southern College was an exotic commission for the practice, but then McAslan has something of a history of searching out interesting commissions in the countries he visits. In this instance, he was driving through the far southern states when he took the opportunity to see the largest complex of buildings anywhere by Frank Lloyd Wright – a complex that includes one of the most striking of Wright's late works, the Annie Pfeiffer Chapel. The condition of the campus, however, with ten Wright buildings constructed between the

services introduced in a bold manner that recalls McAslan's youthful London rehabilitation schemes. "It was an opportunity", says McAslan, "to work with 'handmade' buildings, learning from them and informing the way we put together our own buildings." JMP's involvement with Florida Southern College continues, in terms of both the repair of the historic buildings and the addition of a new administrative and social centre, the latter seen as a 'gateway' to the campus and described by McAslan as "the first truly low-energy building in all Florida".

For any McAslan project involving historic buildings the starting point is a detailed assessment of what exists. The results of this assessment, which always has a strong input from one of the practice's conservation architects, frequently add significantly to the factual knowledge and interpretation of a building or site and allow the practice to conduct an informed dialogue with planners and historic buildings authorities such as English Heritage. A good example of this approach is the project at Derngate, Northampton. It was a job that John McAslan would personally have found hard to decline given that the centrepiece of the scheme – 78 Derngate – was the only built work in England by Charles Rennie Mackintosh. McAslan had helped found the Mackintosh Society while still a student in Edinburgh in

Unselfconscious constructors:
Jean Prouvé's Maison du
Peuple, Clichy, near Paris, and
Owen Williams's Boots Factory,
Nottingham

the early 1970s, and remembers being awestruck as a child when taken to see Mackintosh's masterpiece, the Glasgow School of Art. In this phase of Mackintosh's (tragically short) career the architect, working from London, was turning in a new direction that contained strong elements of Art Deco and Expressionism but also pointed the way towards a purer Modernism. Although most of the contents at 78 Derngate had been removed, the interest of the house itself remained. John McAslan + Partners (again with Adam Brown as project director) accepted the commission, initially from a local voluntary trust, to prepare a masterplan for the restoration of the house (which is, in fact, a tiny four-storey terraced unit) and the development of two adjoining houses to form an arts and education centre. One of these, number 80, has now been totally rebuilt to provide a series of reception and exhibition spaces and a place where material relating to Mackintosh's work, the history of number 78 and its owner (Northampton engineering magnate W.J. Bassett-Lowke) can be shown. (The conversion of a further house, number 82, will form the final phase of the project.) In the case of number 78 itself, the only way that the house could be made intelligible – and enjoyable – for visitors was by restoring and replicating many elements that had been destroyed or removed. This approach challenged conventional historic buildings lore, which insisted that the past should never be re-created. A wonderful record of the house as built existed, in fact, in the form of a series of photographs apparently taken by Bassett-Lowke himself – though the fact that they were in black and white limited their value when it came to reinstating original colour schemes. As Sarah Jackson, one of the conservation architects at John

McAslan + Partners that worked on the scheme, argues, "The project had to balance authenticity and practicality – a slavishly purist approach would have led to nothing being done at all."

The practice's research involved collaboration with the Hunterian Museum in Glasgow and the Victoria and Albert Museum in London as well as extensive archival investigation. Fabric research was commissioned from acknowledged authority Mary Schoeser. Paint scrapes revealed a certain amount about the original décor: "There's a story for every surface in the house", says Jackson. Furnishings, fabrics

and wallpapers were reproduced, their patterns transferred by means of digital technology from historic photographs, but only where firm evidence existed as to their original form – nobody wanted to fall into the 'Mockintosh' trap. Project director Adam Brown believes that the use of colour in the restored interiors will surprise many who are accustomed to a black-and-white view of Mackintosh, but he also believes that the project has significantly advanced knowledge of the master's late work ("We're certain that the bedroom reconstruction in the Hunterian Museum, for example, is incorrect in many respects", he declares.) For John McAslan, number 78 is such a precious artefact that "restoration is, for once, justified – much as you might restore a damaged Old Master painting".

McAslan tends to get excited when he discovers fine historic buildings rotting and abandoned – a coal mine in South Wales or a mill in Leeds, for example – when their potential is really so obvious. Despite his passion for history, replicating the past is

investment in the £20 million project. Norman commissioned John McAslan + Partners in 1998 to prepare proposals for repair and conversion. The central idea behind the scheme, that of retaining the great internal space as a performance venue accommodating up to 3500 people, was universally welcomed, but keeping the historic structure free of new insertions brought difficult challenges. The building had to be made freely accessible to all. Space had to be found for additional performance areas, bars, cafés and offices as well as support services. The client's acquisition of a former car park just north of the Roundhouse opened the way for a new structure to house these facilities. This was an obvious solution; but what was not obvious was how to approach its design – particularly in terms of its relationship with the original structure. The resulting 'galleria' building has a boldness that evokes the spirit of its neighbour, with no sign of an over-obsession with lightness. The new addition extends and enriches the original as well as providing the vital additional space, thus ensuring that the original structure remains uncompromised. Stripping away, in this instance, is reinforced by the process of extending.

John McAslan has a great admiration for unselfconscious 'constructors' such as Jean Prouvé and Owen Williams, neither of whom were architects. Asked which living architects he admires, he cites Renzo Piano, Rafael Moneo and Jean Nouvel. Glenn Murcutt's transformation of the Australian vernacular into a new architecture that "touches the ground lightly" has been another enthusiasm for

not normally the McAslan way. There are projects in which the scope for new interventions is limited – for example, the refurbishment of Ernö Goldfinger's listed Trellick Tower flats in west London (although the practice has insisted that it carry out a masterplanning study for the estate in which the Tower stands as part of the exercise). There are others where substantial interventions are vital. The Roundhouse in Camden, north London, is a historic railway structure, latterly famous as a venue for rock music and experimental drama, that had defied a number of attempts at reuse (and was regarded as being 'at risk') before it attracted the attention of inventor and philanthropist Torquil Norman. His vision of a performing arts and music centre for young people attracted support from English Heritage – which subsequently used the building as a venue for the launch of its annual report – alongside the Arts Council and the Heritage Lottery Fund. Together these organizations have taken up the challenge of Norman's own large financial

some years. McAslan's interest in engineering, the expression of structure and the honest use of materials, alongside his fundamental rationalism, separate him from advocates of an architecture of pure form. The perennial concern for fine detail that characterized the Rogers office remains a preoccupation. Concern for detail can, in some hands, lead to a certain preciousness, a tendency McAslan personally seeks to avoid. "You have to build – sometimes a project ends up less than one hundred per cent perfect", he says. "Taking on jobs is a matter of potentially selling your soul to the devil, especially when you are dealing with changing methods of procuring projects or with clients whose aims are uncertain, but you have to take the risk if you want to get things done. In the end, architecture is about making a difference to the world." For McAslan, it is the clients' attitude that can make a real difference. "It's inspirational to work with clients like Torquil Norman or Luigi Maramotti [of Max Mara], who have a cultural vision and a commitment to quality. It's good clients, and we're lucky to have had a number of them, who make the job worthwhile. With those clients who don't share our aspirations, we go as far as we can to turn them round.

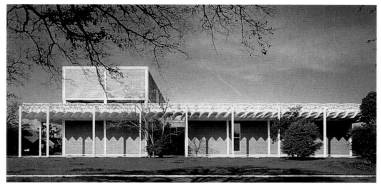

Sometimes, of course, we fail and that can be dispiriting." Clients, conversely, frequently find McAslan's enthusiasm infectious and particularly like the way in which he has created a practice that can balance ideals with a grasp on practicalities. The chief architect of John Lewis Partnership, the client for the Peter Jones project, praises the firm for its ability to "think flexibly when it comes to stuff like the relationship of the old and the new and the spaces in between". Luigi Maramotti of Max Mara recalls that John McAslan + Partners' competition submission had a sense of "belonging to the land; it provided a more urbanistic than architectonic approach". The McAslan way, says Maramotti, is in tune with the Max Mara philosophy – a concern for the "well designed" that incorporates "a close and strong element of functionality". Max Mara, he adds, "is more Louis Kahn than Frank Gehry, and this is reflected in our work together and in the project developed for the headquarters".

Themes and Ideas

It is the rational and practical core to its architecture that drives John McAslan + Partners' approach to designing new buildings. For Max Mara, the inspiration of the site – close to the dense but green city of Reggio Emilia (the perfect urban form of which McAslan admires greatly) – was all; in some respects, the new office/warehouse campus revisits themes that Palladio explored in his farmyard villas. At the Yapi Kredi Operations Centre in Istanbul it was the dense, socially interactive mesh of the Near Eastern city that provoked the idea of internal streets that have a social as well as a climatic role. The St Catherine's College Institute in Kobe, Japan, and the small but exquisite school in Christopher Place, London, are strongly Kahnian in spirit, as is the addition to the Roundhouse. The US inspiration in McAslan's work, indeed, runs deep. Skidmore, Owings & Merrill's Inland Steel Building in Chicago, for example, provided a highly relevant exemplar for McAslan's office tower at Fenchurch Street in the City of London. Kevin Roche's breathtaking Ford Foundation Building in New York is clearly evoked in the designs for the Yapi Kredi Headquarters in Istanbul. Clarity of diagram is something that has always had a strong appeal for the McAslan studio and is a common thread that runs through many recent projects from the office – the Sure Start Lavender Nursery in south London, for example, and the proposed engineering building at the University of Southampton. The poetry of architecture flows on from the logical process of addressing the practical brief. If an exemplar of this truth were needed, it could be found in the work of Louis Kahn, whose Jewish Community Center

in Trenton, New Jersey, is a project that McAslan has revisited on many occasions. In the early 1990s, McAslan worked on a repair scheme for the Bath House, the only part of the Community Center to be built, seeking to reverse the decay of its concrete-block walls and timber roof. Both the Max Mara Headquarters in northern Italy and the Yapi Kredi Operations Centre, situated on the Asian side of Turkey, draw clearly on the Trenton diagram.

The Max Mara Headquarters and the Fenchurch Street tower are probably the most representative of McAslan's recent new-build projects. Max Mara is significant on many levels. First, it is easily the largest scheme that the practice has completed

Clarity of diagram: Max Mara
Headquarters and Louis Kahn's
Trenton Bath House, New
Jersey

over the centuries but still with the tightness and informality of a medieval city. The new, jewel-like city park that the project creates across the road from Fenchurch Street Station is a precious amenity. The building itself is, on one level, straightforward and a response to a demanding commercial brief. It ingeniously adapts a 1950s office diagram to the changed needs of a new century. The strength of the project derives, however, from the ability of the McAslan team to squeeze out of that brief the element of quality that sets the building apart from the general run of City offices. Equally impressive is the way that it eschews obvious display – with SwissRe and Lloyd's Register nearby, another City landmark was not called for – in favour of an elegant and refined contextualism. The historical roots that inspire the practice's work are evident (though the influence is subtly expressed) in both Fenchurch Street and Max Mara, while each is also a highly innovative piece of contemporary workplace design.

In those McAslan projects that involve the reuse or adaptation of historic buildings,

to date. Secondly, it is notable as a sophisticated integration of architecture and landscape in a context – in farmland adjoining the A1 autostrada – where too often the relationship between the two has been ignored in favour of an apparently random sprawl. Finally, it is a project that addresses the cultural, as much as the physical, context – it is no accident that the client is a company with deep roots in the city of Reggio Emilia and its surrounding region, still working its farmland as well as catering to an international fashion market. The scheme reflects a vision of the workplace that looks beyond Italy but at the same time is tailored to local traditions. At its heart is a very Italian view of the relationship between city and country. At Fenchurch Street, in a project of equal gravity, the context is the dense urban mesh of the City, radically reconfigured

it is often the straightforwardness and common sense of what the practice proposes that win favour with the decision makers. At first sight, the King Charles Building at Greenwich, part of the magnificent Royal Hospital complex, posed a huge challenge for Trinity College of Music, whose successful bid to convert the building as part of a comprehensive programme of reuse for the entire site led to the appointment of John McAslan + Partners. The building was not only listed Grade I but also had the status of an Ancient Monument – which meant that English Heritage would scrutinize in detail any proposed alteration. It helped that the building had been through many changes (as was underlined by the practice's research): its original fit-out had been completely removed after the hospital

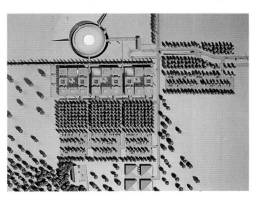

designed by McAslan director Andrew
Pryke) and a new landscape setting unifying
the disparate elements on the site.

These two projects are, however,
exceptional. The typical educational project
of the 2000s has to be delivered to a tight
schedule and a strict budget, with a high
degree of flexibility and low running costs.
In response, the practice has developed
something of a common design approach –
a matter of "rigorous language and carefully
controlled scale", as McAslan director
Murray Smith describes it – for its
educational work. The Sure Start Lavender
Nursery project in Mitcham, south London,
for example, is a low-budget (£1.4 million)
building in an ordinary outer suburb,
though with a pleasant parkland setting.
(The last building on the site was destroyed
by fire.) It had to be tough, secure,
inexpensive and quick to build – a six-month
construction programme using prefabricated
components. The result could have been
a utilitarian structure, whereas what has
been created is something with an element
of delight and certainly of welcome.

The law faculty at Manchester
Metropolitan University (MMU) is a work on
an altogether larger scale, some 6000 sq m
(65,000 sq ft) in area. The same rigour of

closed and the Royal Naval College took
over in Victorian times, and there had been
much reconstruction following fire and
bomb damage in the twentieth century.
Everything of significance in the surviving
interiors was identified and retained.
Fortunately much of the existing internal
space lent itself easily to the creation of
modern teaching and practice areas – the
organizational diagram developed for the
music college responded to the original
diagram of the building. The 'frank'
exposure of services, which lends a special
character to much of the interior, is in tune
with English Heritage's preference for new
work that is visibly an addition to the
original fabric and, in theory at least,
reversible. The success of the Greenwich
project – which was all about the process
of "stripping away, revealing, extending
and enriching" that John McAslan sees as
central to the practice's work on existing
buildings – perhaps helped John McAslan
+ Partners secure a commission in 2003
to prepare a masterplan for London's
Somerset House, an outstanding historic
complex originally designed as government
offices but steadily being colonized for
educational and cultural use.

Education buildings feature strongly in
John McAslan + Partners' current portfolio.
They range across the board, from nursery
spaces to university commissions. Some
are conversions and extensions of existing
buildings and sites, as in the case of Trinity
College of Music. In the case of another
famous London music college, the Royal
Academy of Music on Marylebone Road,
relocation was out of the question – the
academy was determined to stay in the
handsome Ernest George building into
which it had moved in 1911. Since then it
had also taken over a Nash terrace (rebuilt
after war damage) on adjacent York Gate,
but the college remained pressed for space
and needed new rehearsal, recording and
library accommodation. JMP's masterplan
has reconstructed the York Gate terrace
as archive, museum and teaching spaces
and provided a new auditorium in the gap
between York Gate and the Ernest George
building – Pierre Chareau's Motherwell
Studio on Long Island was a typically
unlikely, but appropriate, inspiration for
this structure. The final phases of the
development plan will give the academy a
new library (another skilful piece of infilling,

diagram and close integration of structure and services, however, applies. The development of the project was not, by any means, straightforward. An original scheme planned for the site had to be redesigned and for a time the whole project was in doubt. The brief was rewritten and the redevelopment of MMU's All Saints campus, with buildings of variable quality from the 1960s and 1970s, now has a phased programme over the next decade,

with McAslan set to lead more projects on the site. As a result of the new brief, however, McAslan's building has a very confined site, hemmed in by the noisy Mancunian Way on one side and with only a narrow presence on Grosvenor Square to the front. The new building, which was completed within a contract period of a mere fifty-five weeks, is envisaged as a first phase of development. The main service core is set apart (as in JMP's earlier Fenchurch Street office tower) but not overly celebrated, ready to link up with the next phase of development on the campus. The plan of the building makes optimum use of natural light on the tight site, with a full-height atrium at its heart, within which the lecture theatres sit. The atrium is also the social heart of the building, with its great 30 m (100 ft) long yellow leather bean bag running its entire length. This is a high-value, quality building, unashamedly a new-style piece of 'teaching plant' rather than an ivory tower. In the future it could readily be adapted for purely office use or to accommodate a different mix of functions. For John McAslan, "MMU epitomizes difficulties we regularly face: little money, a limited site, a complex brief, a tight schedule. But the experience has been very useful for us – we see MMU as a key project in many respects." Perhaps the greatest achievement of the project was the way in which it invents a context for the building while giving MMU a 'heart' that it previously lacked.

Setting up a studio in Manchester was a bold move for John McAslan + Partners, and one that was made possible by the MMU project. Manchester has the liveliest

architectural scene of any British city outside London, with large established commercial practices supplemented by the newer wave (represented by Stephen Hodder and Ian Simpson, for example) and new buildings by such international stars as Tadao Ando, Daniel Libeskind, Michael Hopkins and Michael Wilford. John McAslan's instinct, however, was that there was work to be won in the North-West; moreover, "Manchester was the only British city, outside London, that reminded me of Glasgow, but with rather more openness and verve." The small, but growing, Manchester studio, established in 2003 and run by Tony Skipper, has an increasing number of jobs in hand: a performing arts centre in St Helens, an art and design building for South Trafford College and a transport interchange for Piccadilly Gardens in central Manchester. These are relatively modest projects but McAslan, for whom Manchester is "a creative challenge, like starting over again", believes firmly that such commissions are worth taking on and doing well. The high-density, residential-led, mixed-use St George's Island scheme, by contrast, is a very large project, which involves creating a new urban quarter on the edge of Manchester city centre. There is also the prospect of a number of masterplanning and design projects as part of Allied London's mammoth Spinningfields development, off Deansgate. John McAslan + Partners' Manchester office looks set to establish a major presence and reputation in the region.

Transport infrastructure is another sector where JMP is experiencing a substantial growth in its workload. John McAslan feels that projects such as its Crossrail Paddington scheme (a station for the proposed new cross-London rail link) and the reconstruction of King's Cross mainline station demonstrate that "we can take on the largest jobs and compete for commissions with the best". The practice

has considerable experience in the transport field – the booking hall and platform buildings at Redhill Station, Surrey, was an early project (1989–90), somewhat reminiscent of the work of Charles Holden. The Acton Training Centre for London Underground remained unbuilt, but Troughton McAslan, led by Jamie Troughton, was subsequently selected by Jubilee Line Extension (JLE) chief architect Roland Paoletti for several projects on the line. The station at Canning Town, with its complex stacked interchange between Underground, North London Line and Docklands Light Railway, was one of the most challenging JLE commissions. McAslan comments: "This is Jamie's finest work to date, in my view, and it shows him as an architect/engineer of the highest quality."

Troughton McAslan was also involved in a number of support building projects on the JLE, notably the staff facilities at Stratford Station, designed in a rigorous, formal manner influenced by Italian Rationalism and the inter-war stations of Angiolo Mazzoni. A formalist strain, reflecting a particular interest in the Free Style tradition, was present in a number of early Troughton McAslan projects – the shortlisted competition design for the Indira Gandhi Arts Centre in Delhi (1986), for example, and the Alexander House

development in south London (1989). This formalist element now seems to have been expunged from John McAslan + Partners' work.

John McAslan expresses a personal taste for such strongly expressive buildings as Erich Mendelsohn's Einstein Tower, Jørn Utzon's Sydney Opera House and Eero Saarinen's TWA Terminal at John F. Kennedy Airport, alongside a suspicion of architecture where form seems to be achieved at the expense of function and reason. JMP director Murray Smith is anxious that the practice should further explore the potential for integrating architecture and engineering in an innovative way, not to produce striking form for its own sake but in order to "unlock space". Smith, whose training began at Glasgow's Mackintosh School, worked on the Canary Wharf building during his year out and after his diploma (at the University of East London) returned to the practice.

Expressive form: Jørn Utzon's
Sydney Opera House, Erich
Mendelsohn's Einstein Tower,
Potsdam, and Eero Saarinen's
TWA Terminal, JFK Airport,
New York

One of his first completed jobs was the
Christopher Place school in Camden, a
small jewel of a scheme that included a
comprehensive fit-out designed by the
architects ("Getting the most out of a small
project like this is something we're good at",
he argues). The adaptation and extension of
the library at Imperial College, London, was
considerably more complex, involving a very
tight (24-month) schedule, with the building
remaining in use throughout. Today, Smith's
'roving role' in the office includes many of
the urban projects that he finds particularly
satisfying – he is heavily involved with both
King's Cross and Crossrail Paddington.
Both projects are likely to produce
landmark buildings, but the aesthetics are
not the point: these must be structures that
orientate, rationalize and organize, making
sense of transport hubs that are vital to the
future of London as a world city.

New Directions

Murray Smith points to the mixed-use
project for the former Seager distillery site
in Deptford as exemplifying many of the
office's strengths. The scheme includes
the refurbishment of existing buildings on
the site, but also the construction of a
striking 26-storey residential tower, a
proposal that involved detailed discussions
with English Heritage and the Greater
London Authority. The scheme, Smith says,
led to other major housing and mixed-use
projects, including those still in progress at
Oval Road, Camden Town (where offices
and apartments surround a central glazed
'winter garden') and Lodge Road, St John's
Wood, as well as the St George's Island
scheme in Manchester.

In the winning competition scheme for
the Kelvin Link Bridge in Glasgow, which
spans the valley of the River Kelvin between
Glasgow University and the Art Gallery
and Museum, Murray Smith worked with
engineer Tony Hunt to produce a proposal
that was made possible only with the
application of twenty-first-century CAD
technology yet looked back to the history
of the site. Three major exhibitions had
been held at Kelvingrove Park (in 1888,
1901 and 1911). In the 1911 exhibition,
an 'aerial railway' had carried passengers
across the valley in a car suspended from
cables – historic pictures of this remarkable,
long-dismantled structure fascinated the

JMP/Hunt team. Another inspiration was
the extraordinary 'treetop walk' created by
architects Donaldson + Warn in South West
Australia, a system of elevated walkways
that weaves its way high in the forest
canopy. The objective at Kelvingrove was
not just to create an easy route between
university and gallery (the latter recently
comprehensively refurbished) but to
celebrate the act of crossing the valley.
In fact, the bridge was itself intended to
celebrate Glasgow University's 550th
anniversary and it is designed to weave
its own way across the less-than-tropical
Victorian park. The bridge – which is yet
to be built – is a piece of infrastructure,
indeed, in the Victorian tradition, making
something enjoyable out of a functional
necessity. "Our interest was in the whole
experience of the place, making new urban
connections and enhancing the city, not
just in constructing an exciting piece of
engineering", says Smith.

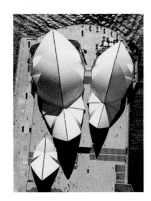

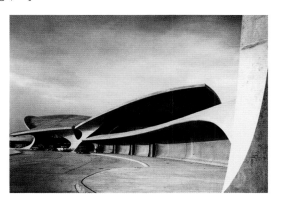

Historic references: Victorian
jute mill, Dundee and Roman
caves at Cumae, near Naples

If the geographical range of JMP's
workload cannot fail to impress – in early
2004 the practice was working on major
projects throughout Britain as well as
Europe, North Africa and China – there is
equally a growing variety and confidence
in its architecture. McAslan architecture
has never been minimal. John McAslan
has encouraged his team to look for
inspiration in unlikely places, be they
Victorian warehouses in Scotland or Roman
caves. New and freer directions in JMP's
architecture were presaged by the project
for a visitor and information centre designed
for the Salvation Army as part of a
development project for the charity's historic
City of London site. John McAslan invited

artist Anish Kapoor to collaborate on the
scheme, resulting in an interior of startling
character – and this long before Kapoor's
monumental transformation of Tate
Modern's Turbine Hall with his *Marsyas*
sculpture of 2002. Meanwhile, a
competition scheme for a new student
union at Queen's University, Belfast, was
strongly organic in form.

The search for strong and expressive
form is also to the fore in the developing
proposals for the new station concourse
at King's Cross. This theme re-emerges in
the proposals for a mixed-use building on
Kensington Church Street – a stone's throw
from JMP's former offices. The site is
close to Notting Hill Gate (a famous location
but visually a great disappointment, with
its run of undistinguished 1960s blocks)
and extends back from the street to the
narrow Rabbit Row behind. In line with
the objective of "unlocking space", the
proposed building meets the ground at just
three points and consists of large irregular
spatial volumes that defer to established
rights of light and views. Above the ground,
structure and skin are integrated to provide
column-free interiors. To develop its ideas
for the site, JMP went to Arup's Cecil
Balmond, the inspirational engineer who
worked with Daniel Libeskind on designs
for the Victoria and Albert Museum's new
Spiral extension. A new route through the
site is provided at ground level, with shops
lining a sheltered square.

The Kensington Church Street design,
Murray Smith stresses, is "highly practical –
a response to the site, not a quest for form
for its own sake. This is a pivotal location,
where raffish Notting Hill meets genteel
Kensington – it cried out for a unique
approach." JMP's credo is to do what is
right in terms of a place and a brief – the
proposal is, in fact, not only visually striking
but commercially astute in terms of the
usable space gained.

Pragmatism and Beyond

John McAslan + Partners is a practice in
transition, certainly determined not to be
bracketed under the banner of 'polite
Modernism'. As John McAslan points out,
"there are too many practices out there
doing buildings that may be efficient and
good value for money but which are entirely
unmemorable and contribute nothing to the
public realm." McAslan's own future role in
the practice could (and probably should)
be that of critic, inspirer and galvanizer of
an array of talents. With an experienced
team emerging, McAslan increasingly has
the opportunity to take up this role. He was
one of a number of young architects raised
in the offices of Rogers and Foster who
formed their own practices in the midst of
the 1980s development boom. All these
firms (and they tended to be double-headed
operations in the Troughton McAslan
mould) were stamped with the now-
discarded 'High-tech' label but none,
perhaps, has succeeded so well in
rethinking its approach to design as John
McAslan + Partners. McAslan believes that
this is the result of laying aside issues of
style in favour of engagement with larger
concerns, including those of history and
context. "Architecture can no longer be
about designing object buildings in
isolation", he says. "Ultimately I see us as
a multi-skilled studio where teams work
together to produce innovative projects of

Idealism in the thinking
process: King's Cross Station
redevelopment

consistent high quality across a wide variety of disciplines." Architecture and masterplanning will always be at the heart of the practice's work, but a range of associated skills – landscape, urban design, conservation and component design – will be brought to bear in unified schemes. It is no accident that so many of John McAslan + Partners' recent projects engage with the landscape, whether rural or urban – the Max Mara Headquarters, King's Cross, St George's Island and the Fenchurch Street office tower are examples. On a number of projects in the past, McAslan worked with the distinguished US landscape architect Peter Walker. More recently, and on the strength of its selection as one of three finalists in the Fresh Kills 'landfill to landscape' competition in New York, the practice has established its own landscape and urban design unit with a brief to contribute to John McAslan + Partners' own masterplanning and architectural projects (as well as to develop its own stand-alone portfolio) and to inform the practice's contribution to the public realm. John McAslan's ambition is to broaden the scope of the office still further, providing space for the contributions of exhibition designers,

film-makers, photographers and writers, for instance, all of whom have increasingly featured in the practice's emerging portfolio. The context to his thinking is a vision of design as a multi-layered, interdisciplinary process. At the same time, architects must, he argues, offer value for money "by holding on to our core values and skills, while responding to change. We can work with standardized components, for example, while still creating something highly individual and special." Designing buildings is only one aspect of the architect's role, however: "We should also be involved in the continuing public debate about the environment and the city – people are not prepared to accept mass-produced, monotonous buildings. Architects must prove that they can offer something extra – innovation, form-making, skill in working in context, for example."

The McAslan office's recent move to a stunning new studio in Princes Place, Holland Park, where John McAslan worked two decades earlier with Richard Rogers, is not just good news for the people who work there (the office at Kensington Church Street had become intolerably crowded). According to Adam Brown, Princes Place reflects "our culture – it's a creative studio, not a conventional office. We work with creative clients – our base should express what we're about." The new studio, refurbished under the direction of JMP's Umberto Emoli, also provides scope for the continuing process of 'opening up' that John McAslan seeks to pursue.

Eight years into independent practice, McAslan has achieved success and the respect of his peers. Personally, he craves new challenges, has a restless streak, and is inspired by projects that are complex and that demand strategic approaches. The charitable trust he has established is active in the field of involving young people in education and the arts in the UK and

overseas, notably North Africa and India. His practice seems to inspire confidence from the commercial sector at the same time as collecting a string of public commissions. Major infrastructure projects are certain to have a considerable impact on it over the next few years. McAslan is not, however, complacent about the practice's achievement to date – complacency is not in his nature: "I tend to question everything about a project", he says. If there is one ambition he nurtures it is to produce work that really does "make a difference". There is a potent streak of idealism in his thinking. Pragmatism, he says, has its virtues – but like patriotism it is never enough.

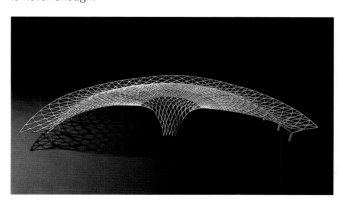

ADAPTIVE REUSE
OF EXISTING BUILDINGS

For John McAslan, working with historic buildings and sites – which may range in date from the ancient Moroccan city of Volubilis to Ernö Goldfinger's late 1960s Trellick Tower, or in scale from a small house remodelled by Mackintosh to a 30,000 sq m (323,000 sq ft) department store – is "a process of discovery and reinvention".

When it comes to working with existing buildings, however, McAslan's particular passion is for the heritage of the Industrial Revolution and the inspirational works of the Modern Movement. John McAslan's personal relish for industrial buildings can be traced back to his childhood on the west coast of Scotland. It is the directness and economy of structures such as the Roundhouse in London or the Sugar Warehouse on Clydeside that he admires. McAslan's interest in the work of such masters as Mackintosh, Mendelsohn, Kahn and Wright has equally had a profound influence on his practice. In no sense, however, is John McAslan + Partners' work on existing buildings, whether listed and iconic or merely potentially usable resources, seen as a specialization or a diversion. Indeed, it informs and nourishes the practice's own architecture. From campaigning to restore Louis Kahn's crumbling Trenton Bath House, McAslan has gone on to design major office and commercial projects in Turkey and Italy that directly draw on Kahnian themes.

John McAslan + Partners' approach to existing buildings is based on an agenda of "stripping away, revealing, extending and enriching". Strict restoration is something it generally leaves to others. But there are few old buildings where restoration alone is enough. Most buildings have to earn their keep and respond to the changing needs of society. Even the De La Warr Pavilion, Grade I listed and one of the finest Modern Movement works in Britain, has had to adapt to survive, developing as a regional arts centre as well as the essentially local cultural and leisure amenity it was when first opened. For the equally renowned Peter Jones store, spatial rationalization and a radical overhaul of services was the alternative to decline and possible closure. The new full-height atrium, which forms the heart of the reconstructed store, is a bold move that challenged conventional conservation philosophy to dramatically successful effect.

The essence of the McAslan strategy is research – establishing what is really important about a building and its site and what is required to renew its life.

Peter Jones has been given a new lease of life but, equally, the building has been redefined in sympathy with the aims of its original architects. This process has taken place equally at Swiss Cottage Library, a 1960s listed building until recently little known and undervalued. John McAslan + Partners' task was partly one of physical repair. More important, however, was that of giving the library an expanded role as a learning resource for the community. An extended dialogue with the local authority (as owner) and with English Heritage saw McAslan's team seeking to balance demands for change with the implications of listing. The result is a building, seamlessly but boldly adapted, that is more heavily used than ever and is increasingly appreciated as a significant work of its era.

Central to JMP's philosophy of conservation is its open-mindedness. Each project starts from first principles. The essence of the McAslan strategy is research – establishing what is really important about a building and its site and what is required to renew its life. Context is all, but there is equally a determination that any new work has a quality and consistency of its own. Literal reconstruction is rarely on the agenda (though on occasions it may be necessary to carry out seamless repair). More often it is a matter of peeling back

the layers of accretion, addition and alteration to reveal the original and make it more legible and comprehensible. In tandem, the space needed for the new interventions that update the building technically and operationally – a transfusion of new life – is unlocked. Here the new elements can develop their own language without compromising the historic quality of the place.

JMP's undogmatic approach precludes hard-and-fast rules, so that the strategy adopted for materials and detailing varies radically from project to project. At Swiss Cottage Library and the Peter Jones store, the interventions made are seamless in that the materials and constructional methods used are those of the original structure. At the Royal Academy of Music, in contrast, there is a clear visual separation between new and old and no attempt to blur the divide between the two.

On occasions, JMP's prescription for revival and renewal may extend beyond the historic building itself. The future of the Sugar Warehouse, for example, is linked to the regeneration of the dockside area in which it stands. At the Royal Academy of Music, new buildings and a landscaping strategy accompany the upgrading of historic structures.

The McAslan approach to history and context is fundamentally holistic: it refuses to recognize old buildings as artefacts to be handled with kid gloves but believes that their destiny is to serve society and contribute to the life of the place in which they stand. Even the most precious historic buildings, JMP believes, can accommodate substantial change if this is well informed, well built and a significant work of architecture in its own right.

JMP's approach precludes hard-and-fast rules, so that the strategy adopted for materials and detailing varies radically from project to project.

HISTORIC SITES
VOLUBILIS SITE MUSEUM
ROYAL ACADEMY OF MUSIC
TRINITY COLLEGE OF MUSIC

VOLUBILIS SITE MUSEUM
MOULAY IDRISS, MOROCCO 1998–2006

The Volubilis project is, by any standards, extraordinary. Volubilis (50 km / 30 miles west of Fez) is the classic 'lost city in the sand': a major centre of population and commercial activity under the Romans (though, in fact, it pre-dated Roman rule), which began to decline in the third century AD. In the seventh century a new Muslim settlement began to grow up nearby, which became the town of Moulay Idriss. A massive earthquake in the eighteenth century – the same quake as that which flattened Lisbon – finally led to the total abandonment of the Volubilis site, which was rediscovered and first excavated only in the nineteenth century.

Since then, much has been uncovered: a triumphal arch, the remains of a basilica, the noble columns of a great temple, and, perhaps most notable of all, the splendid mosaic floors of opulent villas. The excavations continue: this is indisputably the finest archaeological site in Morocco (it was designated a UNESCO World Heritage Site in 1997) and one of the most impressive Roman sites in North Africa. It attracts a steady stream of visitors, in growing numbers – now around 100,000 per year.

Until recently there was no strategy for receiving these visitors and informing them about the significance of the place, which has therefore remained all but unintelligible to non-specialists. Proposals for a visitor centre and site museum have been developed by McAslan as part of a strategy for the management and conservation of the site, which involves archaeologists from London University and the British Museum working alongside Moroccan colleagues under the sponsorship of Morocco's Ministry of Culture. Continuing excavations will explore the post-Roman and Islamic history of the site. Visitors, therefore, need to be informed not only about past discoveries but also about work in progress – much of the excitement of the project lies in what is still to be discovered. Artefacts found on the site, currently housed in distant museums, will finally be displayed at their place of discovery.

John McAslan's involvement with Volubilis began in 1998, when he initiated the project. Several trips to Morocco to meet the Moroccan authorities led to an invitation to develop a project for the excavation and display of the Islamic city that was believed to exist to the west of the Roman city. This programme is now under way and has unearthed extensive ruins dating from the seventh century onwards. It has also led to the preparation of a detailed feasibility study for the proposed visitor building – existing facilities consist of little more than a ticket office and café. Various options for the siting of the new building were explored. In some respects, there was a strong case for placing it to the north of the existing facility, where it would command panoramic views of the whole site and could take advantage of the

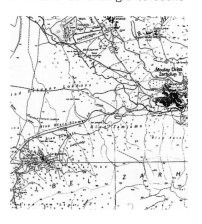

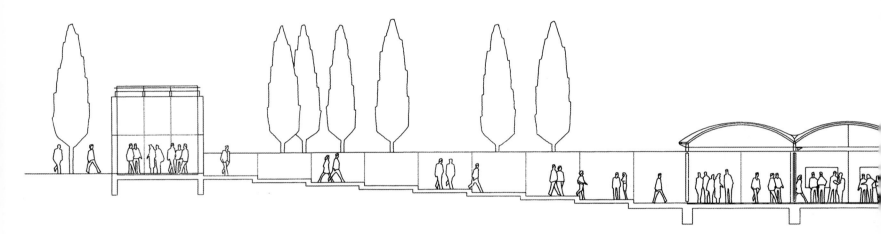

Above and right
Long section and interior view of the proposed museum. The new structure will be sunk into the ground both to insulate it against the heat and to minimize its visual impact on the site.

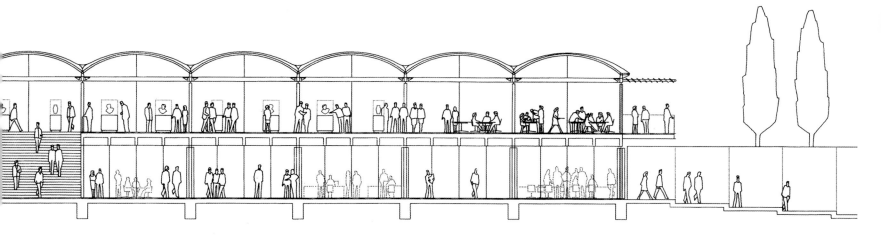

contours in the land to produce some exciting internal spaces. John McAslan + Partners' final recommendation, however – and the selected option – was for the new development to be placed close to the existing complex of research/administrative buildings, where it would have minimal impact on overall views of the historic site and would be screened by a belt of mature trees.

The brief was for a building containing ticket office, café, shop, exhibition galleries, lecture theatre, library and conservation/storage spaces. The 1500 sq m (16,000 sq ft) building will be dug into the hillside close to the ancient wall that encloses the site. It is conceived as a series of stone-vaulted spaces, some open, some enclosed – Kahnian, perhaps, in their inspiration but referring also to the Moroccan vernacular style of construction. Simple in plan, the building culminates in the views from the

double-height display galleries towards the remains of the city. A degree of humidity control will be required in exhibition, conservation and storage spaces, but the mass of the building and use of extensive shading contribute to a low-energy services strategy. This unique project, in which history and modernity interface to a remarkable degree, is now being developed with a view to starting construction in 2005.

Top
Models of the site showing the relationship of the new building to the historic remains.

This page and opposite
The Volubilis site includes the
remains of a Roman temple
and the villas of merchants
decorated with rich mosaics.

Overleaf
Aerial view of model showing
the sensitive siting of the new
museum in relation to the
ancient city.

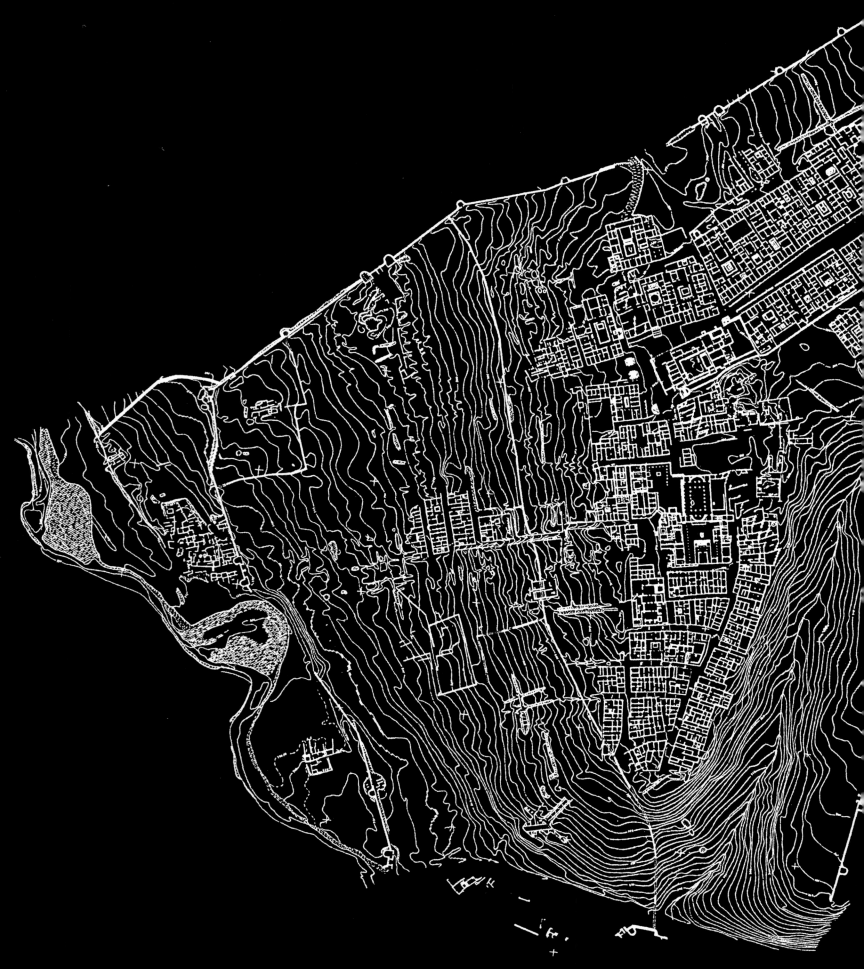

Archaeological Artefacts

Spectacularly sited on a foothill overlooking a broad plain, Volubilis is the most important archaeological site in Morocco, both in terms of its outstanding historical interest and the large numbers of visitors it attracts each year. Working in partnership with the site's conservator, Hassan Limane, University College London (UCL) and the Moroccan National Institute for Historic Preservation have drawn up a strategy for researching, managing and conserving this superb site. Recent work has been supported by UCL, the British Museum and the Volubilis Foundation, headed by Rita Bennis Palmieri and John McAslan.

Although its origins are pre-Roman, Volubilis flourished during the early Roman Empire. The main street was flanked by large houses with colonnaded gardens and elaborate mosaics.

In AD 285, however, the Romans abandoned their Moroccan possessions. At this point the history of the town becomes obscure. It was in a much smaller town that Moulay Idriss, a descendant of the Prophet and the founder of Morocco, was declared the religious and civic leader, or Imam, in AD 789. Site excavations are aimed at discovering as much as possible about the town that Moulay Idriss founded.

Two large areas have been excavated, one in the part of the old town that was still occupied in the eighth century, and one in the new town founded by Idriss I. North Africa's first Islamic baths have been found here, as well as a market, and a large building that may be either the house of an important citizen or a *fundouk* (inn) for traders. Massive amounts of pottery and coins

have also been recovered, leading to new insights into the Islamic city, which brought new house styles, pottery techniques and crops more suitable to the dry climate of North Africa, such as durum wheat.

Important conservation measures have also been undertaken across the site, supported by the World Monuments Foundation. These include the preservation of the splendid Roman House of Venus, as well as the Islamic baths.

Elizabeth Fentress

ROYAL ACADEMY OF MUSIC

Below and opposite
The terrace at York Gate was completely reconstructed in the 1960s. The McAslan scheme has included the refurbishment of this building and the creation of a new recital hall at the heart of the academy's complex.

John McAslan + Partners' phased programme of reconstruction and extension is intended to re-equip the Royal Academy of Music, one of the world's leading music schools, for a new century, addressing the deficiencies of the existing complex while respecting the historic context. Under the leadership of its principal professor, Curtis Price, the academy has secured substantial support from National Lottery funds and private donors to undertake this ambitious project.

The Royal Academy of Music, founded in the early nineteenth century, moved into its current Queen Anne Revival building (designed by Sir Ernest George) on Marylebone Road in 1911.

The building has long been inadequate for the needs of the institution and had generated a number of ad hoc extensions of dubious merit. The academy also occupied premises on adjacent York Gate in the form of a Nash terrace (actually a post-war reconstruction behind the stucco façade).

The project began in 1997–98 with the refurbishment of 1–5 York Gate Terrace (which frames a major axis of entry into Regent's Park) in line with a masterplan by McAslan, which aimed to provide both teaching areas and accommodation for the academy's remarkable collection of historic instruments. These take the form of a 'living museum', and are played from time to time by students and visiting musicians. In the courtyard between York Gate and the George building a new recital hall and recording studio were completed in 2001. Sunk into the ground, this new structure is connected below the courtyard to the other buildings, emerging on the surface as a zinc-clad barrel vault of precast concrete. (The Long Island studio that Pierre Chareau designed for the artist Robert Motherwell was something of an inspiration.)

Developed in line with the masterplan, which provided for the development of the college site as an intense but enjoyable urban campus, the projected new library will occupy a tight slot – the last piece of land available for development on the site – behind the Ernest George building. Day-lit from above and from long windows looking into an internal court, the new block will be clad in textured zinc, uplit by night. The final element in the development project, planned in conjunction with the new library, is a landscape scheme that will act as a marker on the busy Marylebone Road. John McAslan + Partners is also planning a total refurbishment of the main reception areas in the George building in conjunction with this scheme.

The Royal Academy project brings together a number of themes in the practice's work: the refurbishment and reuse of old buildings, a concern for landscape and context, and a flair for new design in a historic context that is both bold and yet appropriate.

Above and opposite
Internal views of the recital hall, showing the rich qualities of natural and artificial light within the space. Timber panelling provides a sense of warmth and contributes to the acoustic performance of the room.

Below
Long and short sections through the recital hall illustrate how it is sunk into the ground in order to reduce the effect of noise from the busy Marylebone Road.

Overleaf
The volumetric quality of the space is revealed by night.

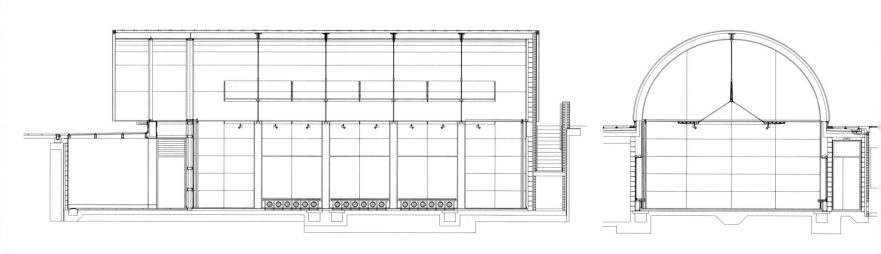

Exhibition Environment

The task of designing an informative installation for a collection of musical instruments forced us to address the fundamental challenge faced by nearly all museums: how do we preserve and protect collections while providing the public with physical and intellectual access to the genius that lies behind them? In the case of the Royal Academy of Music, how do we bring alive exquisitely displayed masterworks of Amati and Stradivari violins and original scores from such composers as Purcell and Elgar for students as well as the visiting public?

Belonging as they do to the oldest *conservatoire* of music in the UK, the academy's assets are more than an outstanding collection of violins, pianos and manuscripts: they have a teaching and performing legacy in which students, composers and players interact intimately on a daily basis.

Positioning the York Gate collection's public rooms adjacent to practice studios facilitates students' movement through the museum, allowing them to engage naturally with the public and providing live experiences within intimate settings. In addition to displays that focus upon the sculptural qualities of the collections, the rooms house workshops for maintaining the historic violins and pianos in playing condition for teaching demonstrations and recitals. Both visitors and students benefit from the opportunity to interact with experts, taking part, for example, in the debate around why in some circles the 350-year-old Italian violins still represent the pinnacle of the maker's art.

In order to ensure that the installations remain fresh and vibrant, the instrument mounting mechanisms and interpretative information are specially designed to be easily altered, enabling curators to embark on a rolling programme of topical installations. In the spirit of the academy itself, the York Gate collection is active and vibrant, facilitating interactions between people, objects and ideas in an intimate atmosphere that is highly conducive to learning.

Phillip Tefft

TRINITY COLLEGE OF MUSIC
GREENWICH, LONDON 1999–2002

Below
The King Charles building at Greenwich provides a new home for Trinity College of Music and is part of the magnificent Royal Hospital complex.

Opposite
McAslan's refurbishment constrasts the monumentality of the Baroque setting with a light and delicate modernity.

John McAslan + Partners' project to provide a new home for Trinity College of Music in the venerable Royal Hospital at Greenwich (itself the successor to the royal palace formerly on the site, which Charles II envisaged as the retort to Louis XIV's Versailles) is a major element in the renaissance of this historic complex.

Trinity College was a Victorian foundation, the brainchild of the Maltese priest Fr Bonavia Hunt who wanted to create an institution open to all – his vision of 'outreach' has a notably contemporary ring. Housed in the West End of London for 130 years, Trinity was one of the

beneficiaries of the decision to close the Royal Naval College, which had occupied the Royal Hospital buildings since 1873. (The Hospital was originally built as a refuge for retired seamen.)

Trinity, led by principal Gavin Henderson, campaigned strongly for space at Greenwich, and after the Naval College vacated the site in 1998 it was allotted the King Charles Building. This had been designed by John Webb in the 1660s but not completed until well into the eighteenth century. The new site allows Trinity to bring together activities previously housed in a number of scattered premises, as well as locating staff and students on a striking campus (three other buildings are occupied by the University of Greenwich). The Grade I listed structure, which is also a scheduled Ancient Monument, consists of four-storey wings around a central court and is part of the finest group of Baroque buildings in Britain. Close consultation with English Heritage was needed to secure consent for the necessary alterations.

The King Charles Building, though externally magnificent, had, in fact, been much altered since the 1870s, with the original, cabin-like rooms (which had been occupied by indigent mariners) stripped out and many routine, sometimes insensitive, alterations carried out internally. A fire in the 1930s and wartime bomb damage, rather crudely repaired, had further compromised the building's internal character. The removal of later additions

was uncontroversial and allowed the architects to provide the practice, rehearsal, teaching, administrative and social spaces that Trinity needed.

The most impressive historic interiors are found in the east wing of the building; these include the stone-vaulted entrance loggia and the former Royal Naval College library, now the Peacock Room. Elsewhere the building was taken back to its bones, with original surfaces left exposed or very simply finished and new services frankly revealed and, in theory, removable (English Heritage wanted new additions to be reversible, although the present somewhat utilitarian approach also reflects a tight budget). Some eighty teaching and practice rooms were created, the latter effectively being sound-proofed boxes kept back from the main structure.

Trinity's Jerwood Library is housed at attic level, where suspended ceilings have been removed to reveal an oak roof structure dating from the 1660s – a 'found' space, it is hugely impressive. McAslan's proposal (supported by English Heritage) to cover the central court with a lightweight glass and steel diagrid roof, forming a social heart for the college, awaits realization in a further phase of works. What has been achieved so far exemplifies the McAslan approach to historic structures: a process of stripping out later accretions, renewing services and extending the buildings' use.

Opposite
View into the dramatic space of the Jerwood Library. The newly revealed roof timbers recall the site's distinguished naval history.

Above and left
The proposed glazed roof structure would create an enclosed central court at the college's heart.

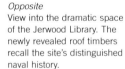

57

INDUSTRIAL STRUCTURES

SUGAR WAREHOUSE
ROUNDHOUSE

SUGAR WAREHOUSE
GREENOCK 2003–2008

The Grade A listed – but dilapidated and seriously endangered – Sugar Warehouse at Greenock, west of Glasgow, a remarkable late Victorian structure, is just one of a succession of threatened historic buildings that John McAslan + Partners has championed, seeking as always to reinforce the historical and aesthetic arguments for preservation with a sound rationale of viable reuse. In this

instance, the challenge is a daunting one but the rewards could be great.

The Sugar Warehouse was built in 1885–86 (engineer: W.R. Kinipple) to store unrefined sugar imported from the West Indies. Greenock was at the time the principal British port for the import of sugar, with local refineries processing the raw material on a huge scale. The warehouse stood alongside the then recently completed James Watt Dock, 1 km (⅔ mile) long and one of the largest wet docks surviving in Britain. The dock is now regarded as one of Scotland's most important historic industrial sites, and the massive Titan Cantilever Crane (installed in 1917) is a landmark on the Clyde. The regeneration of the area, with the surviving historic structures retained, is a major local priority and has the support of national agencies such as Historic Scotland and the Scottish Civic Trust (which placed the Sugar Warehouse on its Buildings at Risk Register in 1995).

The Sugar Warehouse is a huge structure, 206 m (676 ft) long, with two four-storey blocks rising above lower two-storey 'sheds', the whole complex designed with loading bays direct from the quayside at all levels. The external

expression of the building's iron frame is regarded as a particular point of interest.

The building has been largely disused since Tate & Lyle vacated it in the mid-1990s, and it had been only partially occupied since the 1970s. Its condition is now rated as "extremely dilapidated" – the deterioration of the roof has led to the progressive decay of the internal timber and iron structure. Indeed, much of the interior is regarded as unsafe for access. The commission from the Phoenix Trust to prepare a feasibility study for the repair and reuse of the building followed a visit to the site by the trust's president, HRH The Prince of Wales, in 2002.

John McAslan + Partners' studies for the building, developed in association with specialist consultants and with the support of the building's owners, Clydeport Properties Ltd and Inverclyde Council, suggest that one obvious option, residential use, is not commercially viable. The briefest

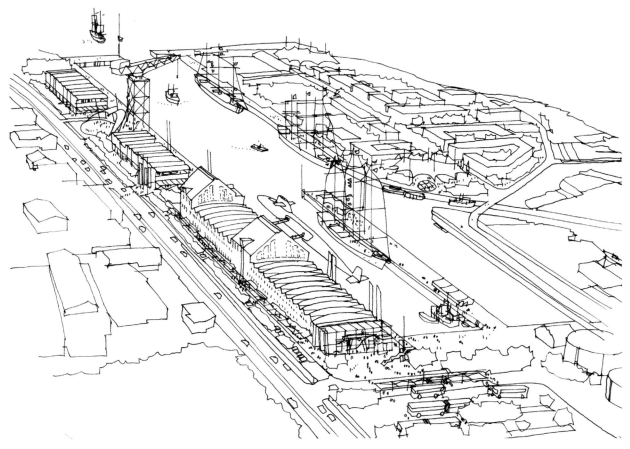

visit to the location, which is hemmed in by a major highway and surrounded by low-value industrial sheds, confirms that this is not an obvious residential site. Merely making the building watertight and structurally safe would cost up to £8 million. In this light, its future looks bleak.

The case for saving the Sugar Warehouse is, however, inseparable from the campaign to regenerate Greenock and other former industrial towns in the region which have missed out on the investment and renewal that has transformed formerly decayed areas of nearby Glasgow. James Watt Dock is seen as a key site in the regeneration process. The emergence of Greenock-based James Watt College, one of the largest and fastest-growing further education institutions in Scotland, as a potential user for the Warehouse could unlock new sources of funding for repair and conversion. The college is

interested in establishing a new 25,000 sq m (270,000 sq ft) riverside campus, which would involve acquiring additional land in the vicinity for further development – the University of East London's new campus in London's Royal Docks provides one possible model. The Warehouse, refurbished to provide 10,000 sq m (108,000 sq ft) of flexible space, would adapt well to the needs of a number of the college's departments and could also house starter units for new creative industries linked to its teaching and research. From being an apparently useless remain, the Sugar Warehouse could be the starting point for a major new educational and employment quarter underpinning, and acting as a catalyst for, regeneration.

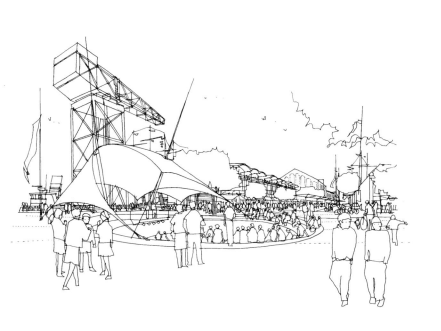

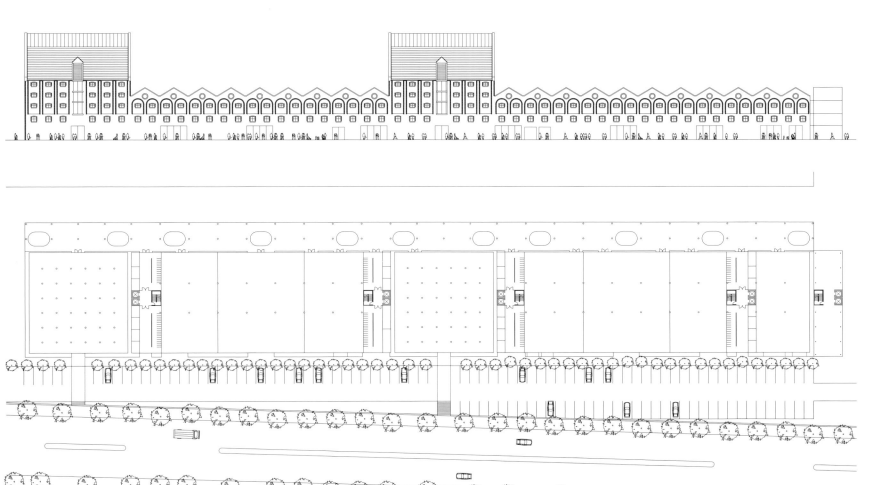

ROUNDHOUSE
CAMDEN, LONDON 1997–2005

The Roundhouse, designed by Robert Stephenson and Robert Dockray and completed in 1846, is one of London's most significant – and, indeed, most magical – historic railway structures, its curved brick walls enclosing a stunning rotunda of wrought and cast iron. Not only is it listed Grade II*, but for Londoners of a certain age it is also remembered affectionately as the venue for many rock concerts (Jimi Hendrix and The Who played here) and avant-garde theatrical performances (such as Peter Brook's innovative productions of Shakespeare). John McAslan + Partners' £16 million programme of refurbishment and extension, scheduled for completion in 2005, will give the Roundhouse a new identity as a performance space and creative arts centre targeted at London's young people. Music, television and video, dance and fashion design feature in the portfolio for the centre.

The Roundhouse project was launched and partly funded by inventor-turned-philanthropist Torquil Norman as a non-'precious' place where youngsters could be encouraged to develop their performing talents; additional funding has come from central government and from Arts Council and Heritage Lottery funds. Norman sees the Roundhouse as having an informal ethos, where young people can genuinely come 'off the street', as well as being a base for more organized educational projects. In order to make the project self-supporting, the building is likely to be let for artistic and social events – which might be anything from rock concerts to fashion launches.

The Roundhouse was built as a locomotive depot, but within twenty years it had become redundant. For a long time it was used as a gin warehouse. More recently it has been the subject of various abortive proposals for reuse, including conversion to house the RIBA's huge drawings collection. John McAslan + Partners' scheme retains the majestic principal space (at the level of the rail tracks) as a highly flexible auditorium and performance space accommodating up to 3500 people. In line with present-day safety, amenity and accessibility criteria, some significant changes were inevitable. The roof structure, for example, has been reinforced with a layer of insulation to contain noise and has also been strengthened to support lighting and sound equipment with no change to its visual character. The original roof light, long filled in, is being reinstated – with powered black-out provision to allow a rapid change of scenario – along with the central oculus.

The undercroft level, which originally housed nothing more than ash pits for the steam engines, is being adapted to contain a variety of studio and performance spaces. With the support of English Heritage, half of the original radial walls (which enclosed long, narrow and unusable spaces) are being removed to make the new 'creative centre' that will occupy this level. The new spaces will be highly insulated in both acoustic and climatic terms – they do not require air conditioning.

In order to minimize interventions into the historic fabric, it was proposed from the

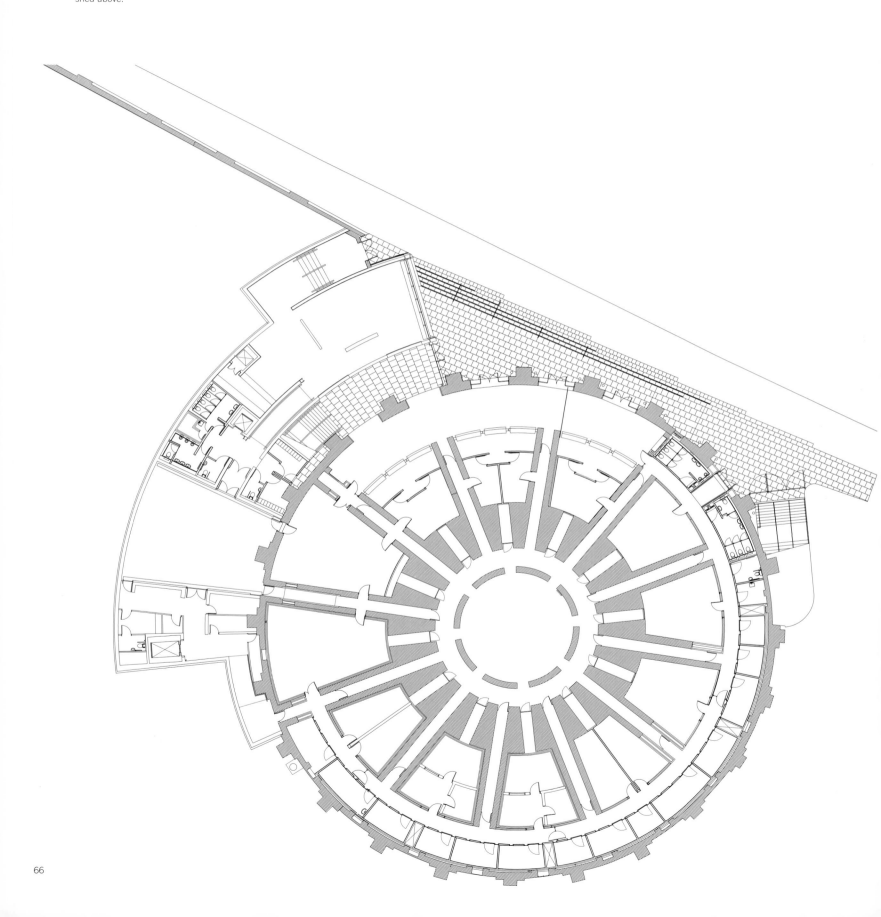

Below and opposite
The contrasting spaces of
the building's two principal
levels are exploited to provide
enclosed studios at undercroft
level and an open performace
space in the former engine
shed above.

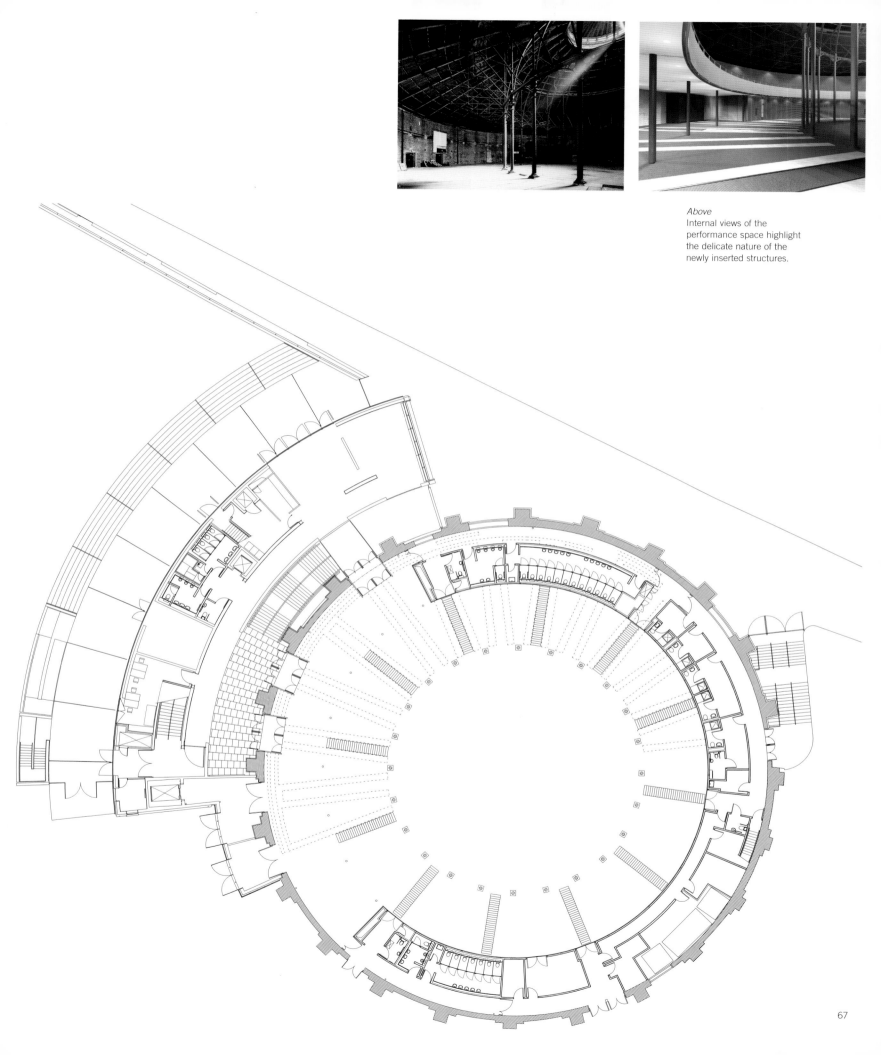

Above
Internal views of the performance space highlight the delicate nature of the newly inserted structures.

Above and opposite
A large-scale study model explores the material and spatial qualities of the new extension wing in relation to the industrial scale of the historic fabric.

Below
The refurbishment of the performance space rekindles the late 1960s tradition of the Roundhouse as a venue for innovative music and theatre.

start that a new building be constructed alongside the Victorian brick drum to contain social and administrative facilities. A number of possible strategies for this new wing were explored but the acquisition of a former car park, just north of the Roundhouse, allowed the present strategy to be developed. The new curved wing, clad in black terracotta and focusing on a full-height internal galleria connected to the Roundhouse by lightweight bridges, wraps around the drum to open up to the street on the south – an inviting extension to a building that was always, inevitably, inward-looking. (Project architect Oliver Wong likens the way that the new building "embraces" the old to the setting given to a precious pearl.)

Working with engineers Anthony Hunt Associates (structures) and Buro Happold (services), John McAslan + Partners has unlocked the potential of a unique historic building of international significance that featured for many years on English Heritage's 'at risk' register. The scheme for reuse breaks with conventional notions of the 'old–new' relationship, whereby each must stand apart and in contrast, in favour of a more subtle interweaving in which historic elements are rigorously protected and new interventions boldly expressed. The revived Roundhouse is likely to become one of the most lively arts venues in London, setting a new benchmark for the sustainable adaptation of old buildings.

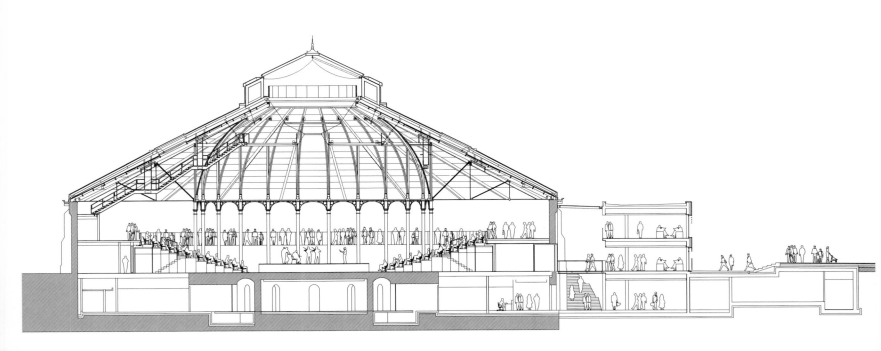

MODERNIST BUILDINGS

FLORIDA SOUTHERN COLLEGE
78–80 DERNGATE
DE LA WARR PAVILION
SWISS COTTAGE LIBRARY
PETER JONES STORE

FLORIDA SOUTHERN COLLEGE
LAKELAND, FLORIDA 1993—2000

Florida Southern College is an extraordinary – and surprising – place. It contains the greatest concentration of buildings anywhere by Frank Lloyd Wright, a fact entirely attributable to the unbridled ambition and relentless energy of former college president Dr Ludd M. Spivey, who telegrammed Wright in 1938 – when Wright was short of work and funds – asking him to assist with the creation of "a great education temple in Florida". Spivey's aim was to expand and diversify what had been a relatively obscure institution: a college founded in 1885 under the auspices of the Methodist Church in order to train preachers and schoolteachers. Wright took on the commission, and over the next two decades ten buildings designed by his office were completed (out of the sixteen planned). The campus is included on the US National Register of Historic Places.

Spivey's sights were set high but funds were limited – and in 1941 the USA's entry into the Second World War resulted in a serious shortage of materials and labour. As a result, some of the buildings were constructed using student labour (paid at ten cents per hour) and concrete 'textile blocks' that were manufactured on site. (This was Wright's first major project using modular blockwork construction since his West Coast experiments with this medium in the 1920s, such as the Hollyhock [Barnsdall] House and the slightly later Storer House.) Within a couple of decades, many of the college buildings were showing serious signs of decay, with the blocks – which Wright predicted would be good for a thousand years – cracking and spalling. A piecemeal approach to repair achieved little.

John McAslan + Partners' involvement with the college began in 1993. A masterplan for repair, reuse and future development was prepared in association with Arup's New York office and locally based architect Lunz Prebor Fowler. The aim was to prepare a phased repair and renewal strategy for the enhancement of Wright's campus, freeing up Wright's structures from later alterations, adding new buildings and reinforcing the landscape setting.

The most important project completed to date on the campus is the $10 million refurbishment of the Polk County Science Center, the last building completed before Wright's death in 1959. The 6000 sq m (65,000 sq ft) building was in poor condition – in part due to the roof, which had leaked badly ever since it was first constructed. The building lacked modern services and did not meet present-day fire safety standards. Its compartmented plan was no longer seen as relevant to the college's teaching, and more interactive and interdisciplinary teaching and support space was needed. A 1960s glasshouse covered part of the eastern façade. John McAslan + Partners' 1996 study suggested that repair and upgrading would cost half as much as a new building of equivalent size; and this was quite apart from the preservation issues that would prevent the college pursuing the demolition option.

The repair of the external envelope formed the first phase of works. Roofs were re-covered

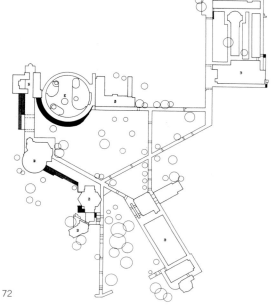

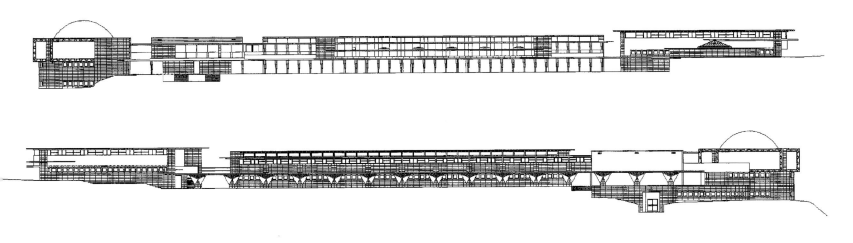

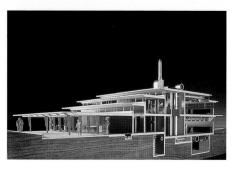

and extensive repairs made to the concrete-block walls. Replacement blocks – made with an amended concrete mix specially designed for long life – were used where necessary, though many of the existing blocks were retained. Internally, the two-storey building was extensively reconfigured, with many more individual staff offices and laboratory spaces rationalized and later accretions, including the glasshouse, removed. New glazed bridges across the central atrium

at first-floor level have greatly improved circulation. The basement level has been much expanded and opened up (there was an existing utilities tunnel) to house augmented services – the ventilation of the laboratories now meets the most stringent safety standards. Service ducting inside the building has been left exposed, the gleaming casings contrasting with Wright's solid masonry, and exposed ducts form a new roofscape; the approach, in line with US principles of adaptive reuse, has been to make services a removable and renewable element separate from the historic structure. The aim was to upgrade the building's services without any loss of usable space.

An entirely new building, the Gateway Student Center, has been constructed in line with the development plan for the campus (see p. 19). Designed by Roger Wu of John McAslan + Partners, this building provides Florida

Southern College with a much-needed 'front door', a social and administrative hub that will free up space in the Wright buildings and permit further refurbishment work to proceed. The building is conceived as an open forum, with a central glazed court between two wings of accommodation functioning as a naturally ventilated space designed to cope with the sometimes steamy Florida climate. The Gateway Center forms a dignified but not over-assertive addition to this classic Modern Movement ensemble.

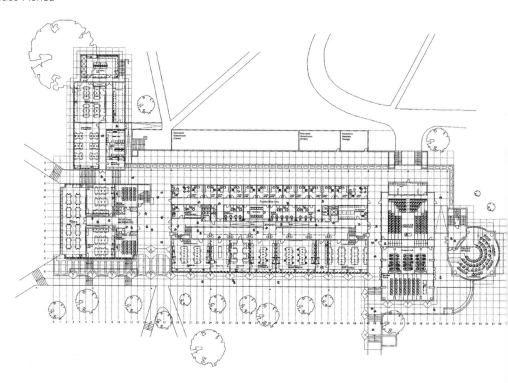

Opposite and this page
The introduction of new services was a major objective of the project, which had to be achieved with minimal impact on the existing fabric. The building's organization along a central spine allowed the effective introduction of a new air handling system.

Overleaf
View inside the Planetarium, perhaps the most distinctive space within the Center and, externally, a notable feature of the campus.

Textile Techniques

Frank Lloyd Wright used his 'textile block' system for all the buildings at Florida Southern College. The system employs large stack-bonded masonry blocks with special grooved edges; these grooves allow horizontal and vertical steel reinforcing rods to be grouted into position in the cavity walls. The result is a structure that is both strong and visually pleasing. The blocks themselves have patterned surfaces – some with coloured glass inserts – with a consolidating dentil design and a shadow groove to camouflage the jointing.

Since their construction, these beautiful and visionary buildings have unfortunately suffered deterioration in various forms. In part this can be

attributed to inappropriate maintenance, but mostly it has resulted from the progressive degradation of the textile blocks. Samples from Florida displayed similar characteristics to samples previously examined from Wright's Freeman House in Hollywood, California. An initial preliminary condition report led ultimately to the decision by the college governors to refurbish the Polk County Science Center, the largest Wright structure on the campus.

Wright probably designed the textile blocks to resemble St Augustine sandstone (the only satisfactory building stone in Florida), and unlike concrete they contain no coarse aggregate. The blocks were manufactured using the 'semi-dry' method, in which the just-damp mixture is compacted into moulds and can be demoulded immediately (like a 'sandpie'). This is a difficult process to control, and the thoroughness of mixing, the

moisture content, the degree of compaction and adequacy of curing all affect the inter-connected porosity (permeability) and hence the durability of the hardened material.

The seemingly congenial Florida climate is actually quite demanding for construction materials, with frequent and significant changes in temperature and extreme cycles of wetting and drying. Such cyclic weathering induces dimensional changes in permeable materials, which can lead to breakdown and disintegration. Moisture ingress through the blocks and via the joints can lead to rusting of the steel reinforcement with cracking and spalling of the blocks.

The aim for replacement blocks was to reproduce the appearance and texture of the originals while reducing the permeability and also establishing quality-control measures to ensure consistent production. Three different Florida sands were selected, and these were blended in proportions to minimize voidage when mixed in a 3:1 aggregate:

cement mix with added pigment, and styrene butadiene polymer emulsion used as mixing fluid. The correct amount of mix liquid was determined from full-scale manufacturing experiments and an effective curing regime and quality-control procedures established. The new blocks are nearly a thousand-fold less permeable than the original Frank Lloyd Wright textile blocks.

John Figg

Below
The Derngate project includes both the faithful restoration of number 78 and the radical reconstruction of number 80.

Opposite
The staircase screen in number 78 extended the full height of the house and was its most important surviving feature.

Number 78 Derngate, Northampton, is the only executed work in England (and, indeed, the last completed work) by the renowned Scots architect Charles Rennie Mackintosh. A radical conversion of an existing terraced house, the project was completed between 1916 and 1919 for the locally based model engineer and art patron Wenman Joseph Bassett-Lowke (who later commissioned Peter Behrens to build New Ways, Northampton, often claimed as Britain's first modern house).

Though it is a late work – Mackintosh died in 1928 – 78 Derngate is one of the most remarkable projects that the great architect completed. The three-storey extension that he added to the rear (southern) elevation – which enjoyed an unspoiled view across the River Nene – is as close as he got to the purity of the early Modern Movement. In contrast, the revamped interiors of the house displayed a dazzling range of decorative themes and moods. Most of the work at

Derngate was completed in 1917, but Bassett-Lowke recalled Mackintosh in 1919 to furnish and decorate the guest bedroom. Here he produced one of his finest interior schemes, comparable with the best of those at Hill House in Helensburgh fifteen years earlier.

Most of the portable contents of the house have long since been removed (the extraordinary guest bedroom furnishings feature in a reconstructed interior in Glasgow's Hunterian Museum, for example). The initiative to restore number 78, and to create a new arts centre in the adjacent numbers 80–82 Derngate, was initally broached by the Charles Rennie Mackintosh Society (of which John McAslan was a founding member while at university in the 1970s). Pat Douglas of the Society was a key mover of the idea in the early 1990s. The project was subsequently taken up by the local authority and has since been progressed by the independent Derngate Trust, led by local benefactors Keith and Maggie Barwell and made possible by a range of public (notably Heritage Lottery) and private funding.

Number 82, which is planned to house additional gallery and support space, was excluded from the first phase of the project due to inadequate funding but will form a later phase of work. Number 80 has been comprehensively stripped out and reconstructed behind its listed street façade to provide access to 78 at basement and second-floor levels – number 78 is a very

narrow and far from large house (originally six rooms on three full floors and one attic floor) and visitor access was never an easy proposition. A glazed display enclosure extending vertically through number 80 contains examples of Bassett-Lowke's model engines and boats, made in Northampton. This is a strikingly bold intervention and something quite unexpected behind a period façade. There is also an exhibition placing Mackintosh's work for the Bassett-Lowkes in the context of his other projects and the broader European architectural scene.

From the beginning, the restoration of 78 Derngate as a visitor attraction raised the issue of to what extent replication and reproduction were acceptable in this historic context (there was no chance of removed furnishings being returned to the house).

Above and opposite
Painstaking research informed
the restoration of the key
interior spaces – the entrance
hall, dining room and guest
bedroom. Decorative features
were reinstated and, where
appropriate, furniture was
reproduced on the basis of
surviving originals.

Sarah Jackson of John McAslan + Partners was responsible for an intensive research programme. This involved the use of surviving photographs, many taken by Mackintosh's client, alongside written evidence (including the recollections of George Bernard Shaw, a friend of Bassett-Lowke – who incidentally kept a bust of the writer on his mantelpiece), collated with the results of paint scrapes and other forms of on-site investigation. Lost wallpapers and fabrics have been replicated in line with recommendations by specialist consultants. Some reproduction furniture has been introduced, though only where originals exist to be copied. The project treads a delicate line between strict authenticity and practicality: every effort has been made to integrate essential modern services in a sympathetic manner. The restoration also extends to the reconfigured garden.

Relatively modest in terms of scale and cost, the project is set to cast new light on Mackintosh's shadowy 'Chelsea' years and question many assumptions about this phase of his career – some critics, for example, see late Mackintosh as linked to the emergence of Art Deco as a fashionable style, yet at Derngate he emerges as a 'pioneer of modern design' in the Pevsnerian sense. The care and conviction with which it has been developed reflects John McAslan + Partners' commitment to historic restoration that is firmly based on scholarly research, and to the integration of history with bold new design.

Opposite and this page
The total reconstruction of
number 80 provides access
to the Mackintosh house at
basement and second-floor
levels via a staircase and lift.
A new display cabinet
extending the full height
of the building houses a
collection of Bassett-Lowke's
models of ships and trains.

Overleaf
An interpretative gallery relates
the history of Bassett-Lowke's
model engineering company
and his patronage of Mackintosh.

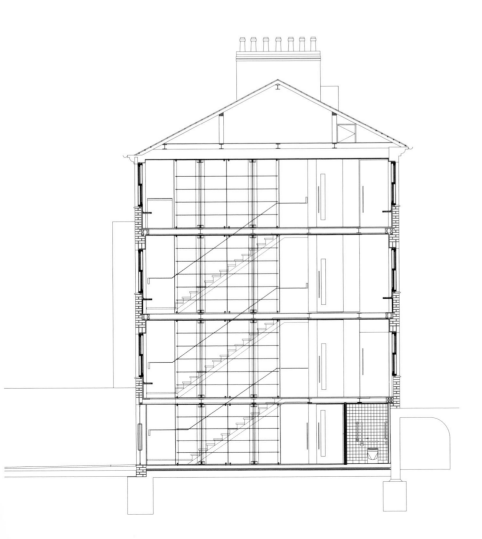

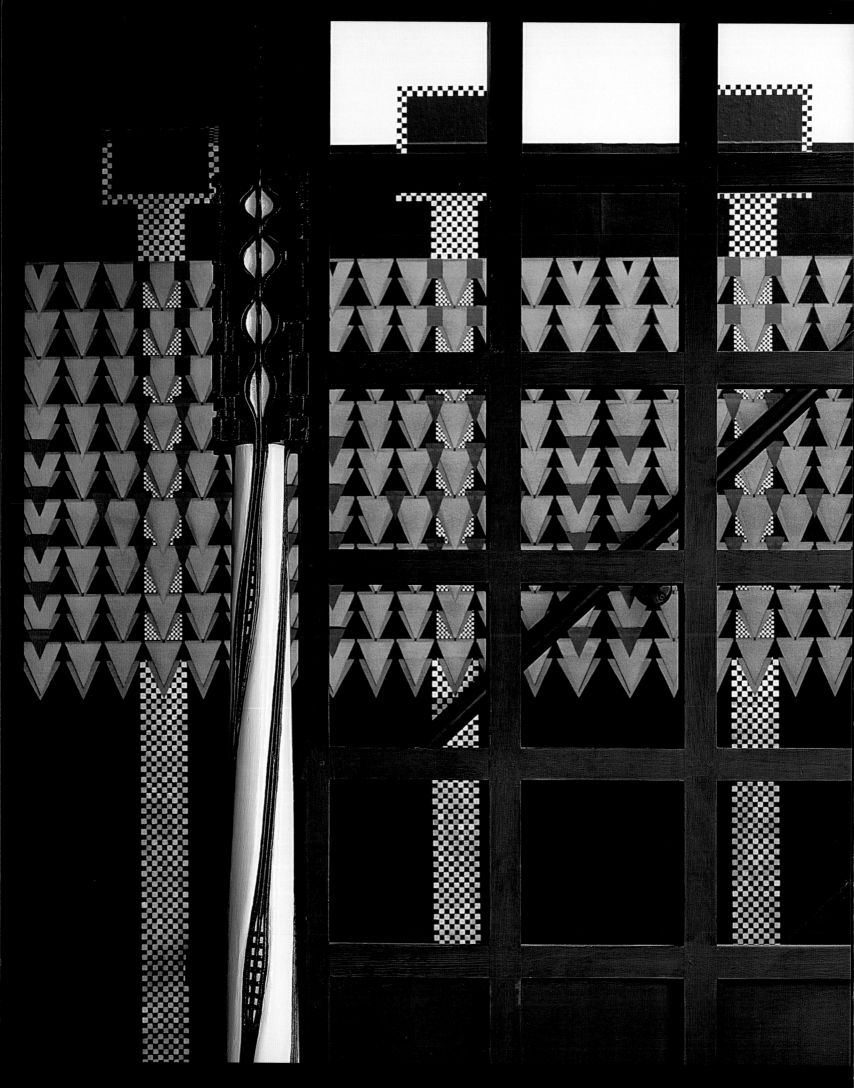

Surface Strategies

Number 78 Derngate is primarily about decoration – about colour, surface and texture. One might also mention Mackintosh's radical architectural interventions – the construction of the rear extension, the relocation of the stair from 'front to back' to 'side to side' and the installation of contemporary services (interventions that served to emphasize the flow of space, fresh air and use of technology, all important later Modernist concerns) – yet the character of 78 Derngate remains rooted in its decorative finishes.

Restoring these finishes set a number of interesting challenges, since little of the 1917 decorative schemes survived in any form. A range of research material, however, was available to work on: physical evidence (the house itself, paint research, surviving furniture), documentary evidence (design drawings by Mackintosh, letters between Mackintosh and Bassett-Lowke, the black-and-white photographs) and conjectural evidence (use of historical and practical 'making' knowledge, general archive material). The restoration project depended on teamwork, coordination, thorough research, patience and a good deal of intuition.

Number 78 Derngate is tiny, but every wall face, floor finish, window treatment and fitting was a one-off, so research was intensive and extremely time-consuming. There was no 'straight' specification or universal approach; everything was unique in terms of both research and production. For each element the substrate, texture and colour 'facts', if any, were ascertained. These were the primary sources but, since little of the physical fabric remained, they were relatively scarce. They included evidence that existed *in situ*: paint samples, stained glass, tiles and inlays on the furniture. Secondary sources, such as the written and oral accounts, generally proved to be unreliable, either for their oversimplification (what kind of blue is blue?) or for the inaccuracy of language (for example, the term 'papered' could refer either to the process of hanging a wall covering or to the substrate of the material itself), but they did help to establish an attitude and enable a 'case' to be put forward. Colours are particularly difficult to describe, since, in addition to the three-dimensional issues of brightness, saturation and tone, they have historical resonances and are affected by personal preferences; the team had to get into the mindset of both the period and the characters involved. Textures suffer even more in written accounts, being rarely mentioned yet essential to the feel of the space. This had an impact on both the research and its practical application. The only way of transferring colour and textural references between members of the team was with actual physical samples: tiny scraps of fabric, paint swatches and wool tufts were passed around, discussed, tested and eventually matched.

The result is extraordinary: a riot of colour and pattern. Once one has gone beyond the initial sensory impact, the textural subtleties can be absorbed, the attention to detail appreciated and the original skill that must have been involved properly recognized. Flat matt paint is used with gloss, cut and loop carpet is laid side by side, and stripes of cotton satin are raised up on a ribbed linen weave – simple manipulation of ordinary things can produce incredible effects. Derngate is a house of drama, but it also has richness and depth.

78 Derngate might feel alien to today's polite tastes, but its approach is absolutely contemporary. Mackintosh worked in Glasgow at the height of the shipbuilding era, when interiors were stripped out and refitted quickly and efficiently, in a choice of styles depending on cost and taste. Mackintosh's attitude to interiors was the same. This image-dominated shopfitting approach is not dissimilar to how we work today: surface strategies dominate the architectural agenda. Cladding, wrapping, layering – the contemporary language is one that Mackintosh would understand.

Sarah Jackson

Below and opposite
McAslan's involvement with the De La Warr Pavilion extends over some years and has led to a major restoration of the Grade I listed building. Although defined by its seaside location, over time the building has suffered from exposure to the corrosive effects of sea air.

A passionate concern to rescue one of the most significant Modern Movement buildings in Britain from decay and decline, and to reinstate it as one of the jewels of the south coast, provided the initial impetus for John McAslan + Partners' long involvement with the De La Warr Pavilion at Bexhill-on-Sea. The practice, with director Adam Brown leading the project team, took up the cause of the pavilion as long ago as 1991. At this time the future of the Grade I listed building was extremely uncertain, and it was the subject of a restoration campaign by the local charitable trust (led by tireless campaigner Jill Theis). The costs of repairs to the structure (which had fared badly on its exposed shoreline site) and to the failing services, as well as much-needed improvements, were far beyond the means of the owners, Rother District Council. The closure and sale of the building were a serious possibility.

The pavilion, which opened in 1936, was designed by Erich Mendelsohn and Serge Chermayeff as part of a bigger (and unrealized) masterplan for the Bexhill sea front. It was originally intended as a place of recreation, a community centre with a broad appeal: theatre, restaurant, bar, reading room and rooftop games area were provided. The use of a lightweight steel frame, the extensive glazing and the remarkable cantilevered secondary staircase were entirely novel features in a public building in Britain at this time.

The campaign to restore the building, which won the support of the local authority, has enlisted support beyond the immediate district, with a vision of the pavilion as a regional as well as a local facility. As a result, funding has now been secured from the Arts Council and Heritage Lottery for the main phase of works, scheduled for 2004–05. In advance of this, John McAslan + Partners carried out a limited programme of urgent repairs to the envelope of the building and refurbished the theatre and bar area, providing a temporary gallery space. Though comparatively modest, these works helped to revitalize the pavilion and to attract new audiences to performances and exhibitions there. Care of the building has now been vested in an independent arts trust.

The current, and final, phase of work provides a range of remodelled and new elements, including a spacious gallery on the ground floor. The foyer area will be restored, as far as is practical, to its original 1930s layout with a new reception area and bookshop. Upstairs, the

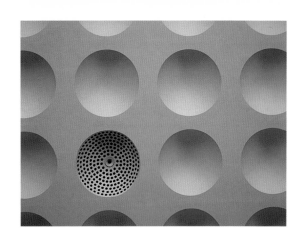

Opposite and above
Restoration of original features, such as the magnificent staircase and the coved theatre ceiling, is combined with the creation of new facilities and the reconfiguration of the landscape around the building.

Below
McAslan's proposals include the refurbishment of the existing pavilion and the provision of new facilities to extend its use and ensure its future survival.

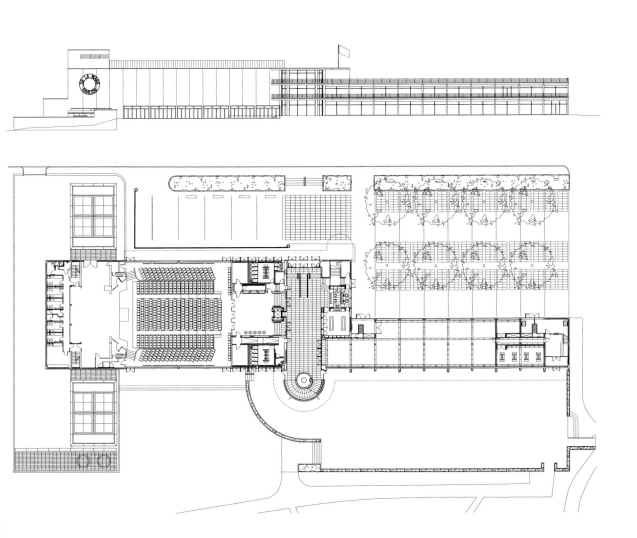

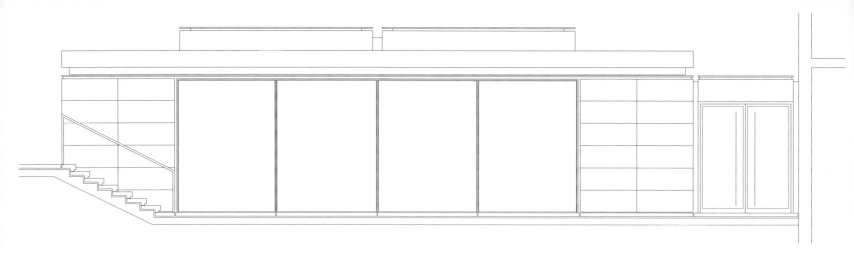

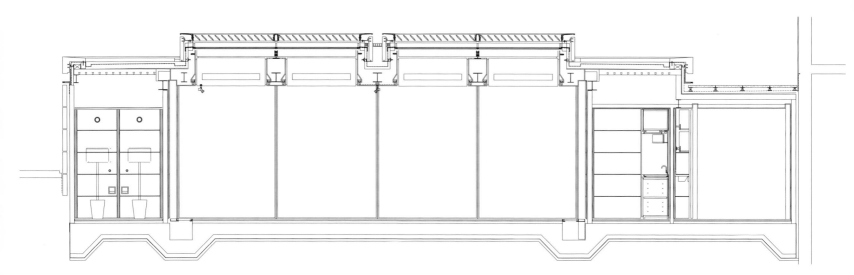

Above
New rehearsal and
performance studios flank
the existing theatre, providing
a community resource for
local people.

extended café/bar and sun parlour area, with its long-lost external stair to the roof terrace, will be reinstated. A comprehensive package of external repairs will address failings in the roof, the external render and the glazing on the south elevation (in some cases windows had been replaced by inappropriate timber casements). Services are being extensively renewed. The flat roof, long closed on safety grounds, will be brought back into public use.

The De La Warr Pavilion, for all its fame, is not a large building. Removing offices from the foyer area means that space for the administration has to be found elsewhere. The idea of extensions at surface level in the form of detached pavilions won support from English Heritage, so offices are now being provided in one of two discreet new wings flanking the theatre. The other wing houses a new community theatre.

Though the budget for the project remains extremely tight, there is every prospect that the pavilion will re-emerge as the landmark structure, a standard-bearer for Modernism, that its founder and architects envisaged.

Left and above
Renovation of the pavilion's east wing will provide a gallery space along the full length of the ground floor.

Overleaf
The future of the De La Warr Pavilion will be secured by a diverse mix of uses.

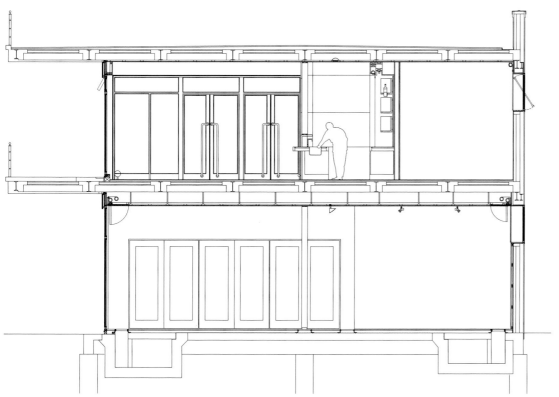

SWISS COTTAGE LIBRARY
CAMDEN, LONDON 1999–2003

Below and opposite
A significant, if enigmatic, work of 1960s public architecture, Basil Spence's Swiss Cottage Library has been given a new lease of life by McAslan's refurbishment project.

Sir Basil Spence's Swiss Cottage Library (built 1962–64) was the work of a partnership that dominated the public building scene during the 1960s with such commissions as Coventry Cathedral, the new University of Sussex and the British Embassy in Rome. The library was one element in a proposed civic centre at Swiss Cottage, to include a new town hall and council offices, designed for the borough of Hampstead. The abolition of the borough – it was incorporated into the new London borough of Camden – killed the civic centre project. Only the library and adjacent swimming pool were built. The latter was demolished a few years ago after proposals to list it were rejected. The library was, however, listed Grade II, heading off possible demolition, and the decision was taken to refurbish it as part of a

redevelopment of the surrounding site. This scheme includes a leisure centre and the relocated Hampstead Theatre, as well as housing and an ambitious public square.

Swiss Cottage Library is not among Spence's best-known works, but John McAslan + Partners' refurbishment of the building (with Richard Ellis as project architect) has underlined its quality. The three-storey library has a rigorous plan, with a clear diagram that makes it readily comprehensible to users – the central atrium is the heart of the building. In developing the project, the architects worked with the client to redefine the role of the building in the light of new technology and the pressure to make libraries accessible and enjoyable to a wider public. Camden's aim was to make the building much more a focus for local community activities than it had been in the past. The library was, in fact, well used and popular, but had a tired and shabby look, while its services urgently needed renewal. Moreover, the southern end of the building was subject to worrying subsidence, with its concrete fins cracking, and had to be extensively reconstructed.

John McAslan + Partners worked closely with English Heritage to develop its proposals. Office and storage spaces are now concentrated at ground-floor

level, with the main public entrance at the north end. Reception and book issue facilities are at first-floor level, where the children's library and gallery are located. A café and learning centre are sited on the second floor (the building has been fully equipped to handle advanced information technology). Around fifty per cent of the total cost of the project, in fact, was spent on renewed services, all of them neatly accommodated without any apparent changes to the building's external appearance.

A key theme in the project has been that of transparency and accessibility. On the first floor, sections of Spence's timber wall cladding have been replaced with glazing, a potentially contentious move that won the approval of

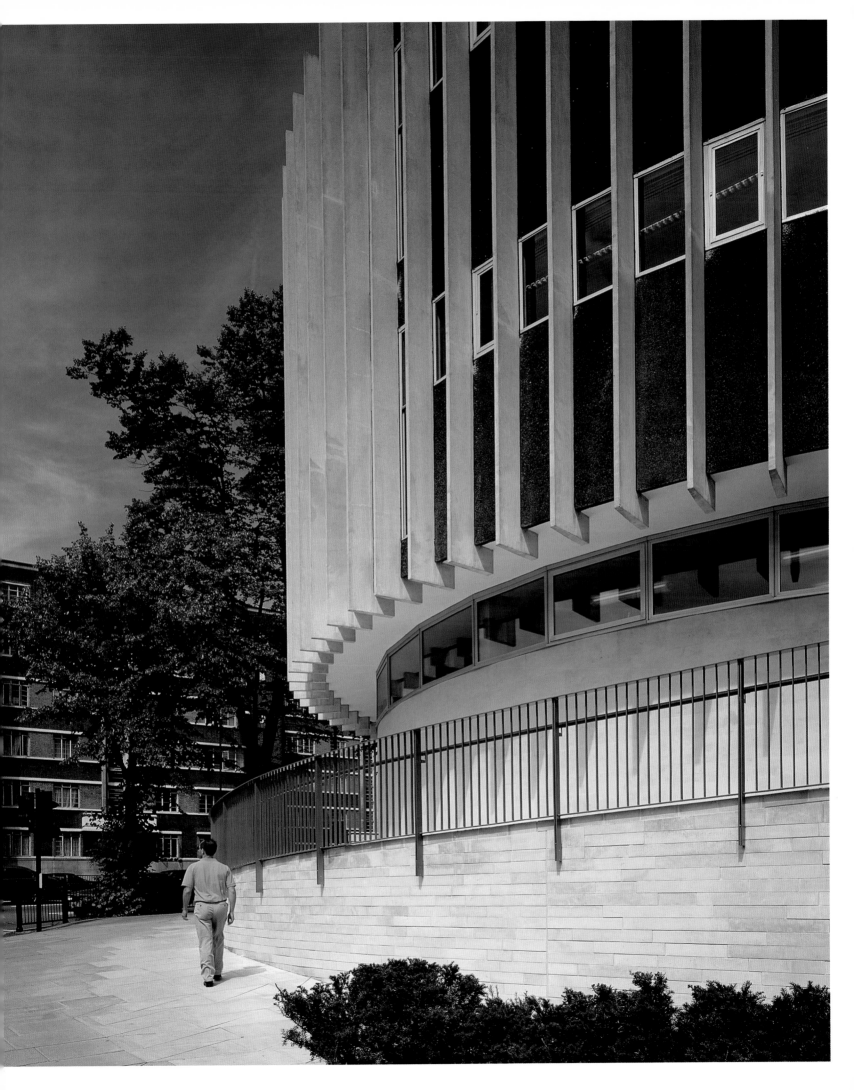

English Heritage. On the floor above, bridge links that formerly contained offices have been opened up as break-out areas, with the café at the centre of the building. Wired glass, standard in the 1960s, has been replaced by fire-resistant clear glazing. Shelving and other furniture is freestanding, providing for flexibility in the future use of the building. Externally and internally, the original materials – a rich and diverse mix, including beautiful walnut doors and the highly practical terrazzo flooring – have been repaired and cleaned. New hard landscaping around the building (designed by Gustafson Porter) reuses quantities of Portland stone salvaged from the demolished pool.

The elegance and rigour of the original building have emerged clearly as a result of the project, and its use has been significantly extended. While this is still clearly a library, it is a facility that addresses the needs of a changing society. The project has demonstrated the potential for updating and re-equipping classic modern buildings while conserving their essential character.

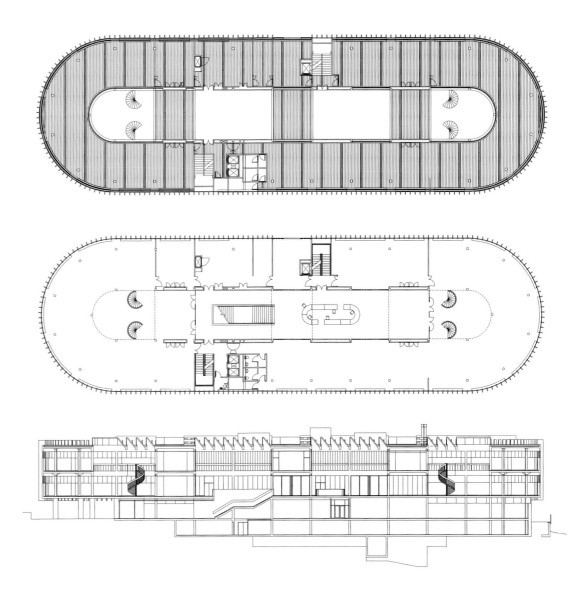

PETER JONES STORE
CHELSEA, LONDON 1997–2004

CHELSEA, LONDON 1997–2004

Below and opposite
A London landmark since the 1930s, the Peter Jones store has been comprehensively refurbished and extended to provide high-quality contemporary retail spaces. A key feature of the project was the insertion, within a new full-height atrium, of escalators connecting all floors.

The Peter Jones department store, at the junction of Sloane Square and the King's Road, is a London institution as well as a familiar landmark. It is, indeed, one of the relatively few modern buildings in London that has been perennially popular over three-quarters of a century. John McAslan + Partners' comprehensive refurbishment and extension of the Grade II* listed store, which lasted over four years with the building remaining in use throughout, has equipped it for many more years of intensive use at the same time as respecting its historic integrity.

The construction of the store (designed by the youthful partnership of Slater & Moberly, working with consultants William Crabtree and C.H. Reilly) began

in 1935. It was halted by the outbreak of war and completed only in the 1960s; remnants of the Victorian store and a fine 1890s house by A.H. Mackmurdo (which would surely have vanished had work not been interrupted for twenty years) were incorporated in the development. As the critic Ian Nairn wrote of the curvaceous curtain wall: "You can see it a thousand times and it will never fail to give a little kick of exhilaration."

Externally unforgettable, with strong echoes of Mendelsohn's department store projects and what is probably England's first true curtain wall, Peter Jones was internally something of a mess, with the various phases of construction poorly integrated and a distinct lack of connection across the site – floor levels varied and the building was inconveniently compartmented. Original light-wells had been infilled to create extra selling space, diminishing the quality of the interior still further. The operational problems of the building, together with the progressive deterioration of its services, led John Lewis Partnership seriously to consider closing the store. Nor was the local planning authority sympathetic to the initial refurbishment proposals, which involved prominent rooftop plant extensions.

Commissioned in 1997 to develop a masterplan for modernizing and re-equipping the historic store, McAslan faced a long period of consultation with

borough planners, English Heritage, the then Royal Fine Art Commission and the Twentieth Century Society. The aim was to create spacious, well-connected modern retail floors within the listed envelope; the retention of historic features (a staff theatre, for example, long disused) had to be balanced against the future commercial viability of the building. A major ingredient of the McAslan scheme was a phasing programme, developed by the architects, that allowed the development to proceed in three distinct stages, with at least two-thirds of the building remaining in use throughout the construction operation. What was proposed was certainly radical, but it also displayed a sensitivity to the historic identity of the building. It was, above all, an integrated solution to its perceived deficiencies with clear benefits not only for its owners and users but also for the wider community.

The £100 million scheme, which started on site in 2000, with the entire store reopened in 2004, has been highly complex but has already transformed the appearance and usability of the building. A new atrium, extending from street level to roof, houses banks of escalators serving all

floors. A top-floor restaurant, with views over South Kensington, is a major feature of the revamped building: it provides a destination at the top of the escalators. The atrium is not just a connector but also a vital element in the innovative services strategy for the building. Major rooftop extensions for plant had been ruled out, so instead air handling is integrated into the façades, with air extracted via vents in the roof of the central void. The very modest plant installation on the roof was made possible through the use of low-energy chilled ceiling beams (unique in a British retail development), which have been painlessly installed within the existing concrete frame. Air-handling equipment is dispersed around the building in ceiling voids adjacent to the refurbished façades, where the air is drawn in through the existing clerestory windows. A store of this size would typically need an entire floor of plant, but this has been avoided and usable space has been maximized.

This project is highly significant in a number of respects. Its services strategy is innovative in satisfying the demand for modern standards of comfort while maintaining the integrity of an outstanding listed building – the façade treatment is a vital element. As an example of well-managed phased construction, which has allowed the business to continue on the site, it is again exceptional. Perhaps most important is the recognition, implicit in the scheme, that it is possible to pick up the traces of an uncompleted project (after forty years in this instance) and realize something of the vision of its original architects by discarding rigidly preservationist codes in favour of a more dynamic approach to the past.

Opposite
A new restaurant provides a
destination at the top of the
new atrium with views across
west London.

Above and right
The floors of the 1930s building
were extended into the surviving
Victorian wing on the northern
edge of the site to create level
access throughout the store.

Overleaf
The extended atrium allows
light to penetrate into the heart
of the store.

STRATEGIC APPROACHES TO NEW BUILDING DESIGN

The agenda that drives John McAslan + Partners' new architecture is inseparable from the practice's philosophy of conservation and reuse: both are design-driven and fuelled by a commitment to sustainability and practicality. Beyond these core concerns, there is a clear aspiration to create new buildings that engage the senses – work with an element of delight, appropriate to its context but equally original and, sometimes, challenging.

McAslan architecture is focused on the development of a practical brief that informs the design, rather than on preconceptions of how a building should look.

The practice's project portfolio is extremely varied, but common themes pervade everything it does: a love of good quality materials; the pursuit of rationality and comprehensibility; a concern for placing a building in its context, whether this be the heart of the City of London or the farmland of Emilia Romagna. Study of the context of a project – physical, social and operational – is an inevitable first stage on the design process. Indeed, McAslan architecture, by its very nature, is focused on the development of a practical brief that informs the design, rather than on preconceptions of how a building should look. It has an internal discipline that is not forced but fundamental to its genesis and, indeed, generated by the functional requirements of the brief. Beyond this, the aspiration to create social space (which can be external or internal) is a key element in all the work, whether commercial, educational or residential in nature.

The practice has been fortunate to work with major commercial clients, such as Max Mara and the Yapi Kredi Bank, on the development of innovative new workplaces that not only reflect the practical needs of those organizations but also embody something of their history and ethos. In a high proportion of John McAslan + Partners' projects, the involvement of an inspirational client has been a factor in the creative process. The practice demands from clients as much as it gives them: every project is a collaboration. Even where the future user of a building has yet to be identified, the architecture can instil an element of inspiration alongside concerns of efficiency and practicality. It is the ability to see beyond the latter that distinguishes JMP's office development in Fenchurch Street, for example, from other recent City projects of its sort. This project embodies a clear concern for public space alongside the core imperative of creating an outstanding workplace.

New architecture must respond to a changing social and cultural climate. John McAslan + Partners' work in the field of education reflects changing views of learning, at all levels from nursery to university. The scale of expansion in provision has generated a need for high-value, flexible and highly functional buildings that share the low-energy, interactive programme of progressive workplace design. The practice is working on a range of projects, each distinctive in terms of the building's function but all reflecting these shared concerns.

In the field of residential building, the studio is developing a strategy of creating places rather than just units. The St George's Island scheme in central Manchester, for example, embodies a thoroughly urban aspiration to forge a new city quarter that relates organically to its

context. As with so many other McAslan projects, the landscape surrounding the buildings is central to the success of the scheme. Landscape, indeed, is seen as inseparable from architectural design. The Max Mara project saw JMP working with landscape architect Peter Walker in response to a client brief that was rooted in the terrain in which the development stands, and in a vision of the harmony between city and countryside.

Working on transport and infrastructural projects is nothing new for the practice, but the commissions to develop schemes for the Crossrail station at Paddington and for King's Cross Station, London's busiest transport interchange, are significant by any standards. It is no coincidence that these projects are generating a radical response from the office. In both cases, the new interventions must be, on one level, bold statements of renewal, worthy to stand alongside great monuments of the first railway age. At the same time, they are concerned with orientating and directing passenger flows and elevating the sometimes fraught process of travel. The proposals that result from this challenge look set to be the most remarkable work of the McAslan office to date.

Increasingly, John McAslan + Partners is exploring, where appropriate, the potential of strong, non-orthogonal form in its work while eschewing the purely arbitrary art of form-making. Projects such as the King's Cross Station reconstruction and the mixed-use scheme proposed for a site on Kensington Church Street offer the prospect

of a broadening of JMP's philosophy to create memorable new urban landmarks. The work of the practice is constantly developing, but aesthetics are secondary to the conviction that buildings must work well, be built to endure, and respond to an environmental programme that acknowledges the impact of architecture on humanity and the future of the planet.

John McAslan + Partners is exploring the potential of strong, non-orthogonal form in its work while eschewing the purely arbitrary art of form-making.

PRIVATE COMMISSIONS
MAX MARA HEADQUARTERS
YAPI KREDI OPERATIONS CENTRE
YAPI KREDI HEADQUARTERS
60 FENCHURCH STREET
CENTRE DE SOLAR

MAX MARA HEADQUARTERS
REGGIO EMILIA, ITALY 1996–2004

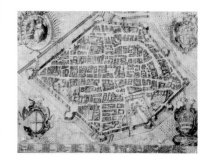

Visiting Italy – a country he never tires of – John McAslan finds delight in sights far removed from the classic cultural attractions. He recalls how, driving south from Milan along the A1 autostrada, he warmed to the raw and expressive qualities of a number of the factories and warehouses built along the route during the 1960s, when 'il boom' was transforming the country. The understatement and elegance that underpin so much of the sense of style for which Italy is renowned are clearly present in John McAslan + Partners' most significant built project to date: the 45,000 sq m (485,000 sq ft) headquarters

development of offices, design studios, showrooms and warehousing for Max Mara. The development occupies a site appropriately close to the A1 autostrada on the outskirts of the historic city of Reggio Emilia. The project, for which Andrew Hapgood acted as project architect, is infused with the rigour that McAslan has made a trademark of his work and which has clear roots in the architecture of Louis Kahn.

Max Mara is a family-owned company established in Reggio Emilia in 1951 by Achille Maramotti. It is now Italy's largest ready-to-wear fashion group, with a workforce of 2500 and one thousand stores worldwide. More than a thousand people work for Max Mara in the company's home town. When the company launched an architectural competition in 1996 for the new headquarters, bringing together activities previously located on a number of sites around Reggio Emilia, it had a clear image of

the buildings it required. In the 1950s, Achille Maramotti had commissioned a distinguished headquarters from the architect Eugenio Salvarani, a member of the progressive Cooperativi Architetti group. The present-day company wished to create a new base of equal quality and, while it deliberately opened the competition to architects worldwide, it was looking for proposals that responded to the distinctive, ordered landscape of the Po Valley, Italy's agricultural

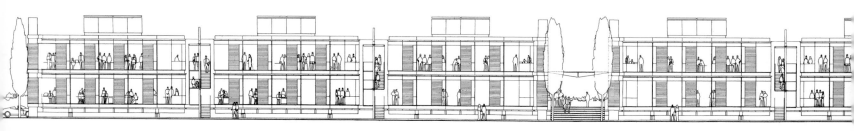

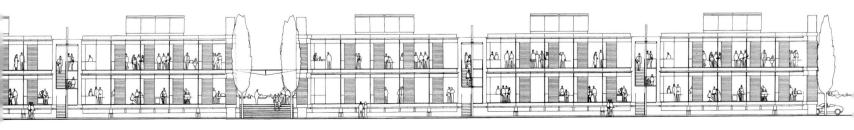

heartland. The Maramotti family retain farming interests and are well-known producers of parmesan cheese – the integration of agriculture and the fashion trade on the site is not just for show.

Luigi Maramotti, chairman of Max Mara and son of the company's founder, has commented that "good designer style is closer to architecture, instilling a culture of working towards the permanent". Max Mara, he believes, aims at design that incorporates "a close and strong element of functionality". Above all, it is an operation with roots in its locality and a sense of local identity. The site, formerly

farmland but metres away from the motorway and a new high-speed rail link connecting Rome and Florence to northern Europe, was seen as embodying that identity. "John McAslan + Partners was the only team that understood that this aspect of the project was the most important part of their submission", Luigi Maramotti says. Most significantly, McAslan's architectural ideas were linked to a landscape strategy designed by landscape architect Peter Walker, and the way in which the two were integrated was the decisive element in securing the commission. The landscape is rooted in an Italian tradition of ordered planting that seems to exemplify a view of the relationship between humankind and nature. Walker recalls the client's "desire for connectivity", and the final landscape design achieves a penetration of the fields' geometry through the buildings and out the other side. The penetration is

achieved via 'windows' of poplar trees which, in fact, become a site element as powerful as the buildings themselves.

The 'family' of buildings on the 30 ha (74 acre) site is arranged on a highly disciplined grid, in tune with the landscape of plantations and irrigation channels (enclosing fields that are still farmed) that surrounds them. The warehouse and distribution building, the first built element to be completed, is a vast and simple container built of precast concrete on a 13.2 m × 25.2 m (43½ ft × 82½ ft) grid. This suitably matter-of-fact structure contains a sophisticated racking and storage

Opposite and above
The Max Mara Headquarters complex, close to the historic city of Reggio Emilia, responds to the orderly context of the Po Valley in terms of both its architecture and its landscape.

Below
The modular diagram of the buildings, arranged on a highly disciplined grid, clearly shows a debt to the work of Louis Kahn.

Left
The offices make use of external shading devices to baffle the strong Italian sun.

Right
An internal street runs the full length of the showroom's elevation.

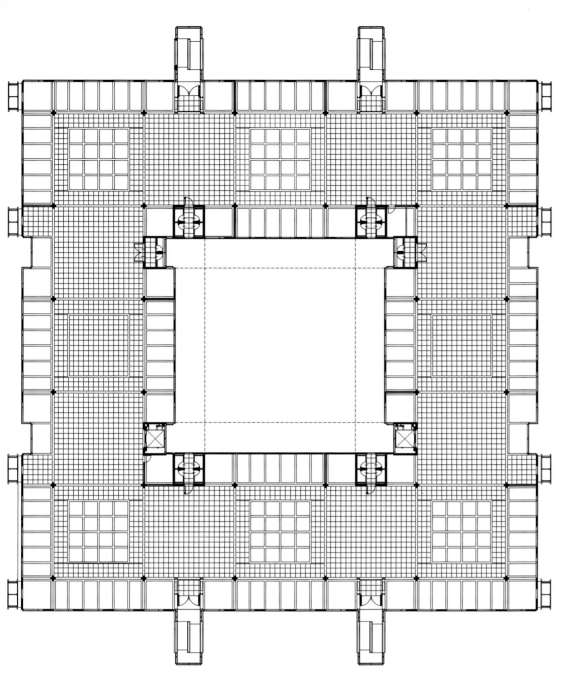

Left
The cellular form of the development is exemplified in the plan of the offices, which are arranged around central courtyards.

Below
Covered entry to the offices also defines the route between the buildings.

system operated by a small number of employees, and is clad with precast panels and a ventilated metallic rainscreen. The strongly articulated stair towers provide a visual emphasis. In contrast, the office complex is broken down into three linked pavilions arranged around internal courtyards, with curtain-walled glazing relieved by metal-framed panels of glass and brick tile – a reference to the building traditions of the region. Internally, the offices are highly flexible, its 3.6 m (11¾ ft) service zones clearly subsidiary, in the Kahn manner, to the 18 m × 18 m (59 ft × 59 ft)

office pavilions. Inside, the aesthetic is equally Kahnian, with exposed concrete contrasted with timber panels – a memory of the Mellon Center at Yale. Studio spaces on the top floor benefit from carefully moderated top-lighting. The cafeteria serving the whole site is a calm, timber-lined space with carefully chosen furnishings located at the southern end of the warehouse and distribution building. There are particularly memorable interiors in the showroom block, where crafted elements contrast with the essentially modular kit-of-parts character of the building. Brick panels are again used, with limited amounts of glazing, to infill the exposed frame of the building.

The grid, along with the use of concrete, gives the entire campus a unity and the feeling of being almost a city in miniature.

There is a subtle sense of hierarchy in this project that is certainly Kahnian, but which equally looks back to the humanistic traditions of Alberti and Palladio. Max Mara is a powerful response to the landscape, as well as an inspired retake on the idea of the workplace, that is both entirely contemporary and imbued with a powerful sense of the past.

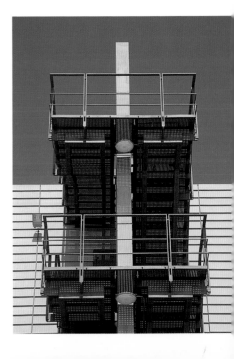

Opposite
View of the warehouse building, a relatively simple, extremely large container that provides automated storage for the firm's products. The canteen is located at first-floor level.

Left
Externally, the building is animated by staircase towers.

Below
The loading docks in the distribution warehouse.

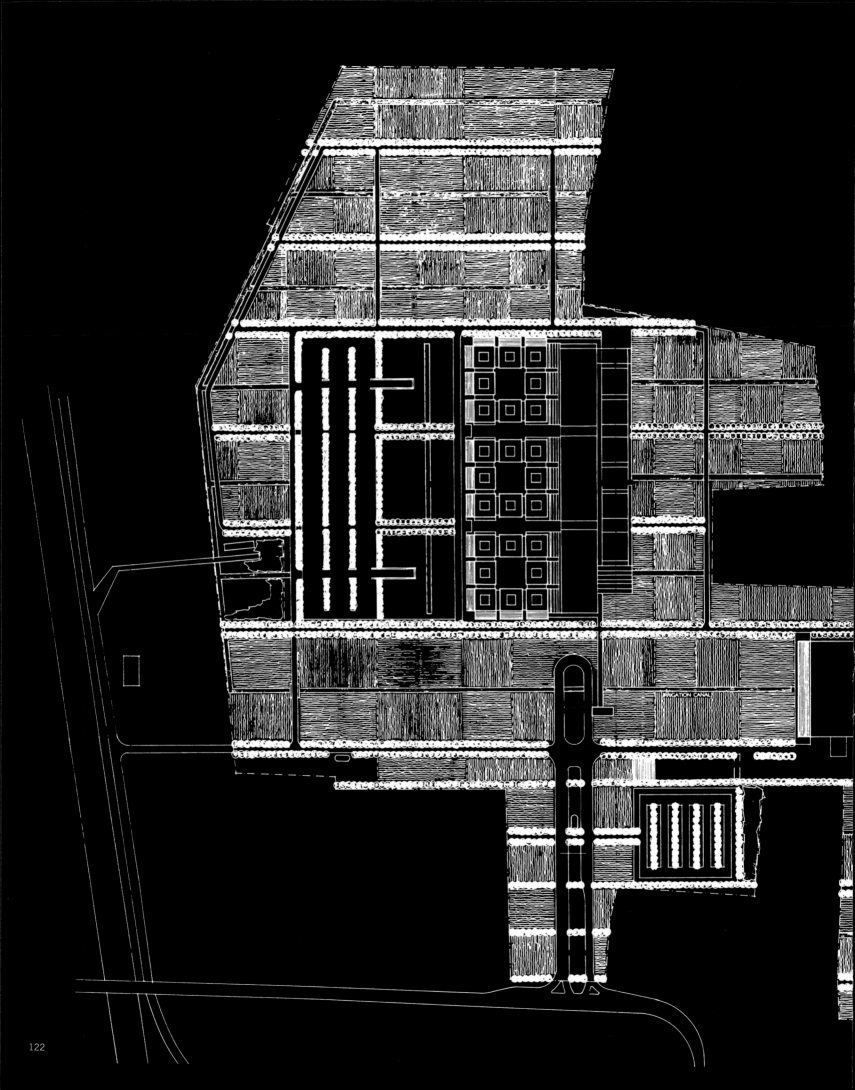

IRRIGATION CANAL

Local Landscape

The landscape concept for the Max Mara Headquarters is a minimalist, pared-down abstraction of the beautiful agrarian landscape of the Po Valley

A constructivist grid of canals defines and scales the fields that spread out and provide the view beyond the headquarters buildings. These canals are working channels that irrigate the fields and also provide nourishment to a series of Lombardy poplar hedgerows. As landscape devices, the hedgerows emphasize the long axis of the site and are drawn from the current irrigation system that exists throughout the countryside. At Max Mara they have merely been composed carefully in order to create a modern villa garden setting.

Lawned terraces reach out from the main building to the showrooms. A border of native grasses steps down to the formal covered parking below The main parking is on grade and is conceived as an orcharded forecourt that includes vehicular entry

Paths of decomposed granite connect and organize all parts of the larger composition while providing comfortable access to the whole garden, in its various scales, for both employees and guests.

The whole finished landscape exists as a place that is at once familiar and contrived.

Peter Walker

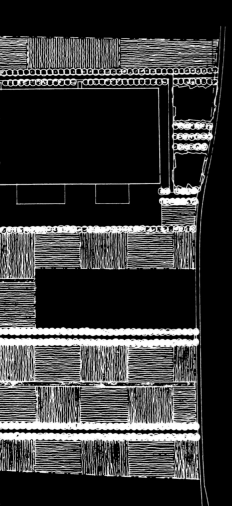

YAPI KREDI OPERATIONS CENTRE
ISTANBUL, TURKEY 1996–1999

Below and opposite
Yapi Kredi Bank's Operations Centre, located near Istanbul, houses 1800 staff in a series of buildings arranged on a molecular plan and connected by covered 'streets'.

Located 50 km (30 miles) outside Istanbul, on a hill overlooking the Sea of Marmara, the Yapi Kredi Bank's 65,000 sq m (700,000 sq ft) Operations Centre forms part of a major development programme by this leading Turkish financial institution that also includes the new headquarters building in central Istanbul designed by John McAslan + Partners (see p. 132).

The Operations Centre belongs within a tradition of innovative workplace design that includes Herman Hertzberger's Centraal Beheer Insurance Co. in Apeldoorn and Niels Torp's SAS Headquarters in Stockholm, but which at the same time responds to the physical and cultural context of Turkey. It houses around 1800 staff, along with the central computer facility, archives, document processing and training centre for the bank. The client brief was for a highly flexible building with potential for future growth and change. On one level, the project can be read in the context of traditional Turkish building – the covered markets and arcades of old Istanbul, for example. (There is a parallel here with Henning Larsen's Foreign Ministry in Riyadh, which similarly makes reference to regional tradition.) Its 'molecular' plan is, however, frankly Kahnian, with structurally independent (this is an earthquake zone), 35 m (115 ft) square, three-storey blocks of office accommodation, each featuring a central court and all linked by internal 'streets' covered either by glazing or fabric roofs. The offices benefit from controlled daylight both from the central courts and from the streets, the latter also acting as a climatic buffer.

Eight blocks were constructed initially, with a further two forming the second phase of the project.

The office spaces are cooled by a low-energy displacement system, in response to the extremes of the Turkish climate, while the connecting circulation areas are semi-climatized 'inside/outside' spaces. Service cores, including vertical circulation, WCs and plant, are kept apart from the main floor plates and are located at street intersections, animating the interior of the building. Glazed lifts and expressive concrete stairs spiralling round the cores, along with bridges providing upper-level

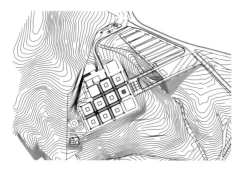

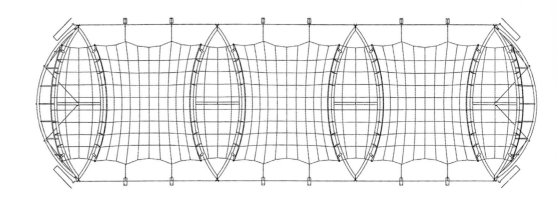

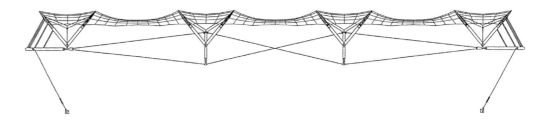

Opposite and above
The internal circulation spaces of the complex are glazed and protected from solar gain by extensive use of fabric blinds and awnings.

Below
The 'streets' are intended as social and interactive spaces as well as a means of circulation.

127

Above
The office spaces, while relatively conventional, enjoy a sense of transparency and connection via the internal 'streets'.

connections, create a dynamic sense of movement and are the lynchpins around which the entire development revolves.

The streets are the essence of the project: they are places for every sort of communal activity, including the informal interaction that is now seen as critical to successful workplace design. To this degree, the operations complex is essentially internalized in character. Externally, it is extremely restrained, the elevations relieved only by sunshading on the east, west and south elevations, yet the architecture is conceived as part of an ensemble in which landscaping and planting, to a scheme by Peter Walker, is fundamental.

Irresistibly evocative of the historic hilltop sites of the Near East, this state-of-the-art financial complex succeeds where many modern buildings in the region fail most conspicuously: in subtly deferring to history while declining to make overt reference to traditional motifs.

Above
A pedestrian bridge provides access to the complex from the parking areas across a valley.

Left
View of the archive and storage area.

Overleaf
Night view of the main entrance, showing the fabric canopy stretched across the access bridge.

YAPI KREDI HEADQUARTERS
ISTANBUL, TURKEY 2002–2006

Below and opposite
The headquarters in central Istanbul for Yapi Kredi Bank focuses on a full-height planted atrium, which is visually intergrated with the landscape scheme for the surrounding site.

The headquarters for Yapi Kredi Bank (for which John McAslan + Partners also designed a highly innovative operations centre, see p. 124) is deliberately conceived as a landmark, reflecting the client's desire for a prestige building with a clear image. The headquarters is designed to accommodate up to 350 senior executives and other staff. The bank was anxious to procure a building with the flexibility to respond to future change in the financial services industry. The brief provided for executive offices, general administrative space, dealing floors and secure storage areas.

The diagram of the 15,000 sq m (161,000 sq ft) building owes something to Kevin Roche's Ford Foundation Headquarters in New York: it features a full-height internal atrium, which is seen as a social and semi-public space, with an exhibition space and bookstore at ground-floor level. The site is the Yapi Kredi Plaza, prominently located on a major highway into central Istanbul; the richly landscaped atrium (and, indeed, the new landscape surrounding the building) is conceived as a buffer against noise and pollution. The headquarters development significantly improves the working environment for the entire complex, which houses around five thousand staff.

The plan of the building is essentially cruciform, with operational spaces accommodated in 16.4 m × 16.5 m (53¾ ft × 54 ft) quadrants, one of which contains a drum core-structure housing lifts, WCs and other services and emerging as an external feature at roof level. The atrium is housed in the north-west quadrant. The building reads as a pure cube. High-performance double-skin façades, incorporating shading devices, add an element of layering that enriches its appearance. Glazed timber screens are separated by a 3 m (9¾ ft) wide landscaped buffer zone from the clear-glazed outer skin – individual users can control the environment of their workspace by using sliding internal screens.

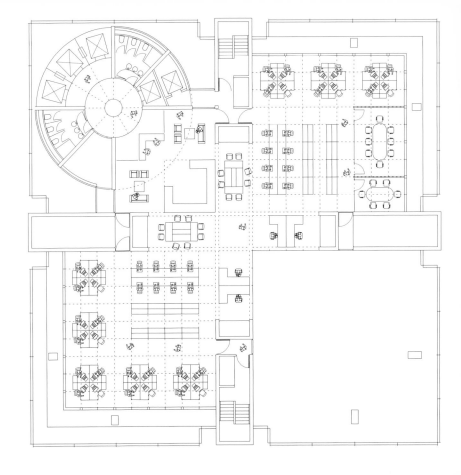

Opposite and above
The organization of the building
is represented by the strong
cruciform plan, which locates
main service risers and stairs
within four massive column shafts.

Below
The volumetric entrance lobby
has a dramatic impact on the
corner of the site and brings the
space of the entry forecourt into
the heart of the building.

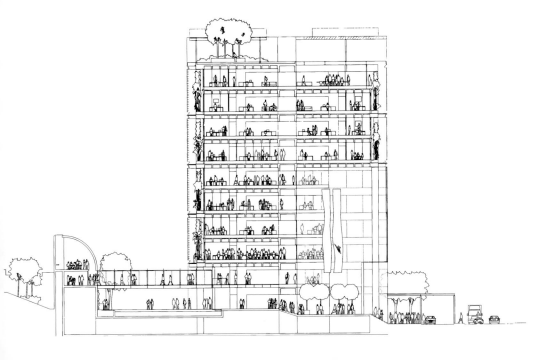

60 FENCHURCH STREET

Below and opposite
McAslan's first City project provides a marker on Fenchurch Street and a connection to the busy commuter station beyond.

The context for this scheme of offices in Fenchurch Street is extremely varied. The Victorian shed of Fenchurch Street Station (overlaid with offices in the 1980s) lies to the south. Fenchurch Street itself is extremely mixed, with few buildings of great quality, but Richard Rogers's Lloyd's Registry of Shipping has made a strong impact on the skyline and forthcoming buildings in the immediate vicinity are set to transform it still further. The wider backdrop includes Rogers's earlier

Lloyd's of London, Norman Foster's SwissRe Tower and the bizarrely Post-modernist Minster Court. Amidst this lively scene, rich in landmark and 'signature' buildings, the calm elegance of McAslan's tower makes a statement of its own.

The roots of the project, which is John McAslan + Partners' first in the City of London, lie clearly in the tradition of rational building developed in Chicago from the late nineteenth century onwards and given a new twist by Mies van der Rohe and his followers after the Second World War. Mies's Seagram Building in Manhattan was, of course, the most famous of the new US office buildings of the 1950s. The Inland Steel Building in Chicago, designed by Bruce Graham of Skidmore, Owings & Merrill, is less well known but has had an obvious impact on the Fenchurch Street project. Though relatively modest in scale (twelve storeys high and 8000 sq m / 86,000 sq ft in area) in comparison with a number of current and forthcoming office developments in the vicinity, McAslan's building promises to be a very positive addition to the City scene.

With major development projects recasting the south-eastern quarter of the City, the need for some public return in terms of open space (always a precious commodity here) and other amenities is obvious. With this firmly in mind, John

McAslan + Partners' project gives the City an attractive 'vest-pocket park' (inspired by Manhattan's Paley Park) in place of the very unmemorable, and distinctly 'left-over', space that previously existed on the site. The landscape of the new piazza responds to its role as both a place of retreat from the streets and part of a pedestrian route to and from the station. It is essentially an open public space, whereas the garden (a former churchyard) that fronts Lloyd's Registry is walled and secret in character.

The new building, which replaces two undistinguished blocks of Victorian and Edwardian date (neither listed nor in a conservation area), takes its cue from the Inland Steel diagram in providing column-free,

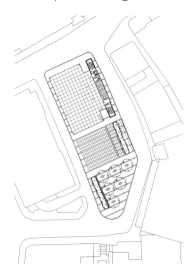

Opposite and below
The highly transparent tower
addresses a newly created
public space, providing a
valuable amenity in the
City adjacent to Fenchurch
Street Station.

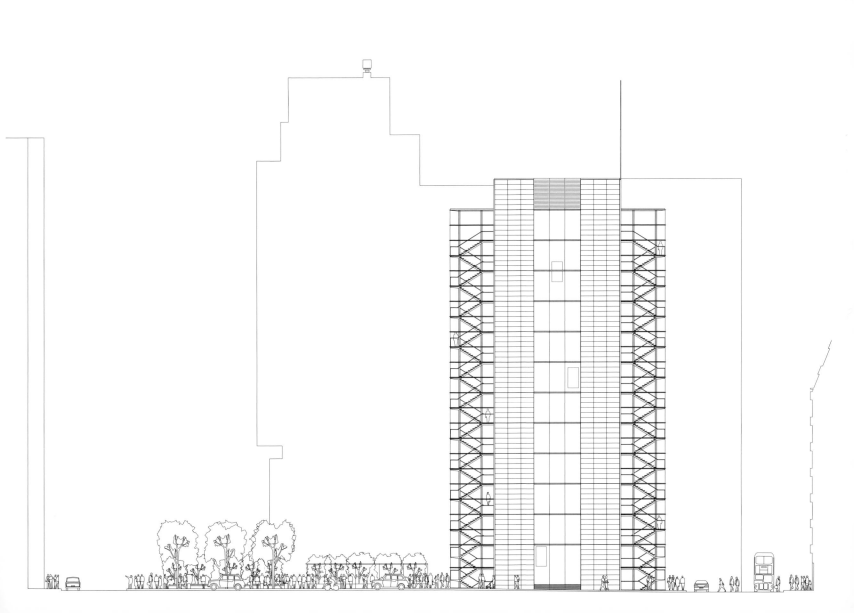

steel-framed 15 m × 27 m (49 ft × 89 ft) office floors with structural support along the edges, and services concentrated in a solid, concrete-framed core zone along the eastern perimeter. The plan of the building is masterly in its clarity and sheer simplicity: an intermediate 3 m (9¾ ft) wide zone connecting the main office floors and services zone forms an entrance galleria at street level. (Most of the ground floor space is allocated for retail use.) Located between the core towers, with their transparent steel staircases, glazed lifts give access to the offices. The building has two principal elevations, to Fenchurch

Street and to the new park; there is no 'front' or 'back'. In the best Miesian tradition, the building aims at maximum lightness and transparency, making use of innovative glazing technology on the fully glazed façades to ensure optimum environmental conditions. Equally Miesian, and ultimately rooted, like Mies's architecture, in Classical traditions, is the treatment of the ground floor as a podium, in this case housing a public zone connecting the main street and plaza beyond. Brilliantly engineered by the late Nick Hanika of Price & Myers (a young engineer who died tragically in 2002), the building is fastidiously

detailed and makes use of a carefully controlled palette of materials drawn together as essential ingredients of the project.

This scheme combines a pragmatic and thoroughly commercial approach with a concern for elegance and urbanity. The result is a jewel-like addition to the City streets and a welcome corrective, perhaps, to the pursuit of extraordinary form that has characterized so much recent architecture in the City.

This page and opposite
In plan and detail, the project draws inspiration from classic American Modernist models, notably Skidmore, Owings & Merrill's Inland Steel Building in Chicago. The clarity of the diagram, however, is characteristic of McAslan's work.

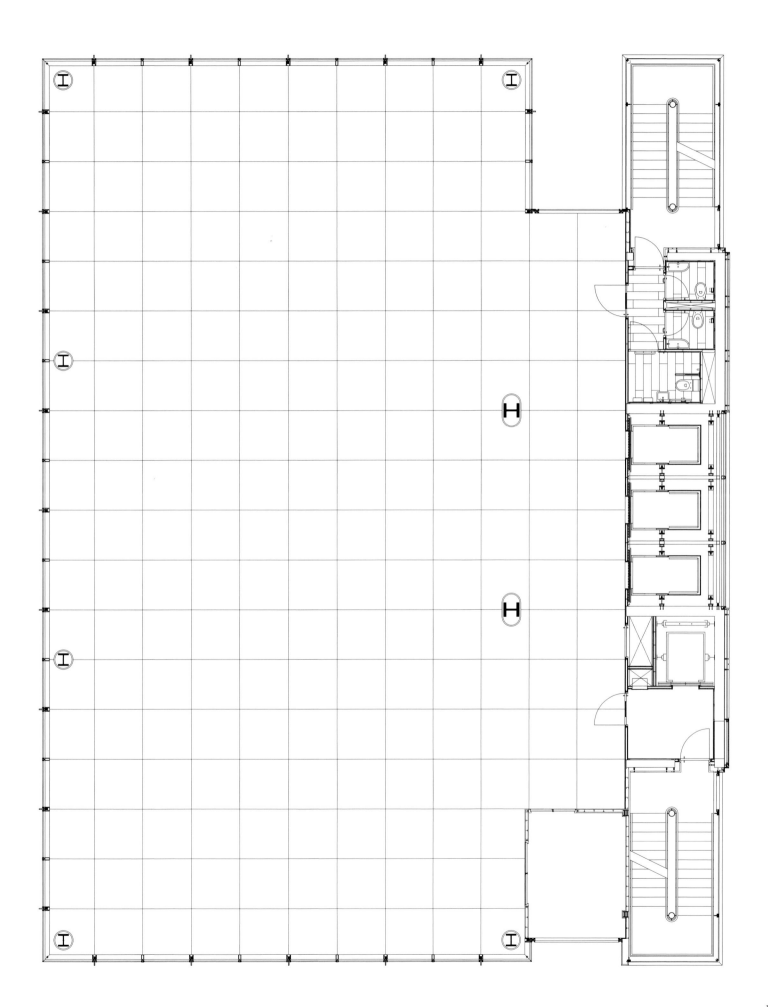

141

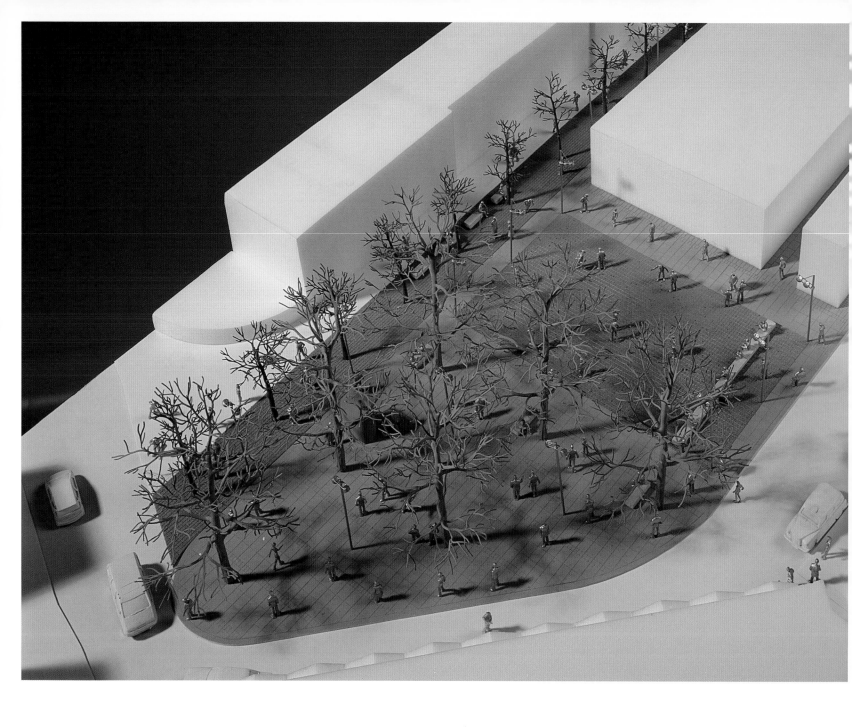

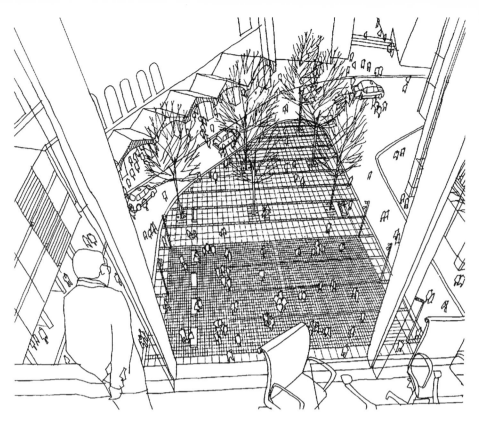

Opposite and below
Fenchurch Place, the first
project realized by the office's
dedicated landscape unit,
forms an oasis of calm in the
midst of the City.

Above
The new space will be
characterized by a sense of
scale and an attention to detail.

Overleaf
The completed Fenchurch
Street building is a calm
addition to the rich and varied
surrounding skyline.

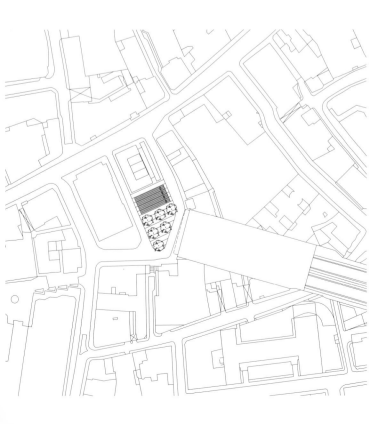

CENTRE DE SOLAR
BEIJING, CHINA 2003–2006

John McAslan + Partners' first project in China includes the masterplan and design proposals for a group of mixed-use buildings as part of a larger masterplan for Centre de Solar, a dramatic new development north-east of central Beijing and adjacent to the city's Third Ring Road. The McAslan proposals, which relate to two of the five zones within Centre de Solar, provide for a 'family' of buildings, focusing on a 180 m (590 ft) 'signature tower'.

Sustainability is a key theme in John McAslan + Partners' proposals, reflecting the growing concern in China for low-energy development. Double-skin façades suspended from the face of the buildings provide a buffer zone against the external climate and thus help reduce energy consumption. The design of the signature tower draws on the history of the site (once occupied by the Sun Palace) and creates a beacon for the development, a symbol of change and renewal. The highly sophisticated, crystalline skin of the tower changes appearance according to the time of day and the season to produce a building with some of the qualities of a living organism. Here, and in the other buildings, the idea of building as lantern is explored. Façade treatments on the various buildings within the 'family' will reflect the identities and preferences of individual tenants, within a common structural and planning grid.

The layout of the site, with buildings around courtyard gardens, responds to Chinese tradition and at the same time creates benign landscaped areas that act as oases from traffic and pollution. Residential development is concentrated to the north, with commercial elements around the signature tower to the south. A retail zone connects the two. The aim is to create an appropriate urban scale of city blocks permeated by pedestrian routes and landscaped areas.

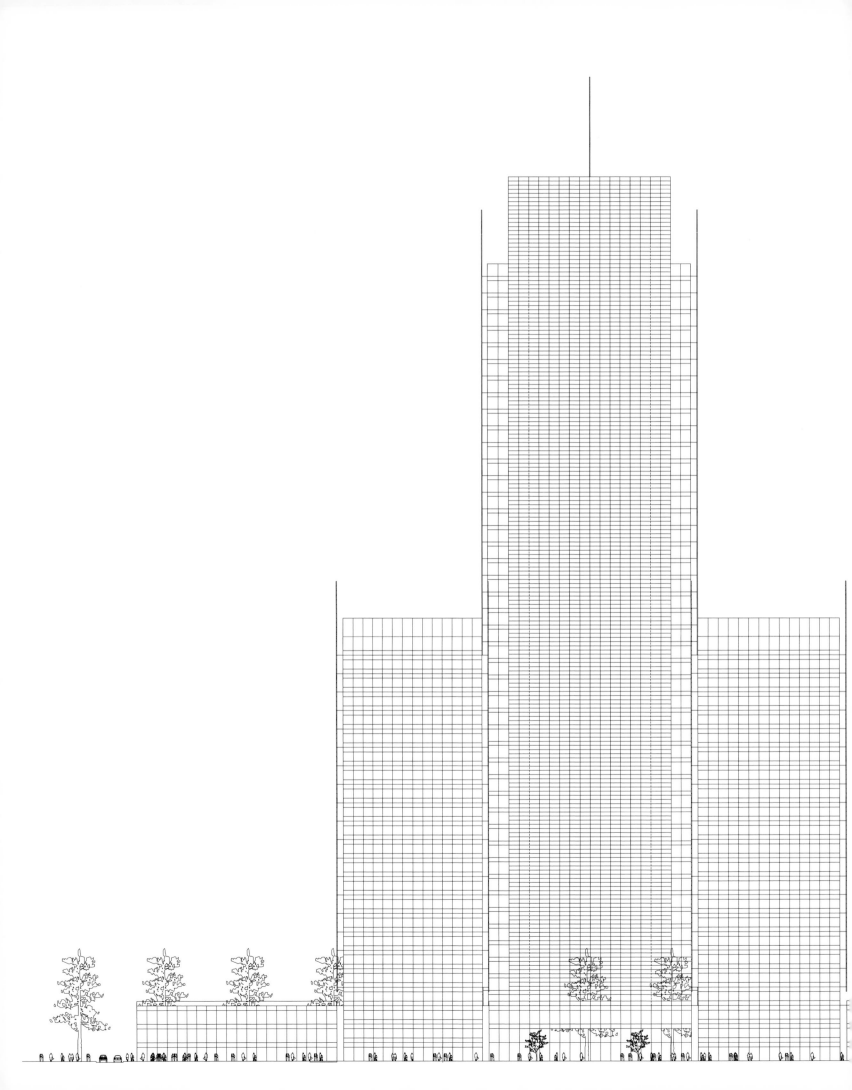

Opposite and above
A signature tower 180 m
(590 ft) high forms a focal point
within the group of buildings.
Their elevations are defined
as suspended screens, inviting
analogies with traditional
images of the 'lantern' as a
beacon and symbol of change.

Overleaf
Centre de Solar is located at the
north-east corner of Beijing's
Third Ring Road, a prominent
site providing high visibility from
various approaches.

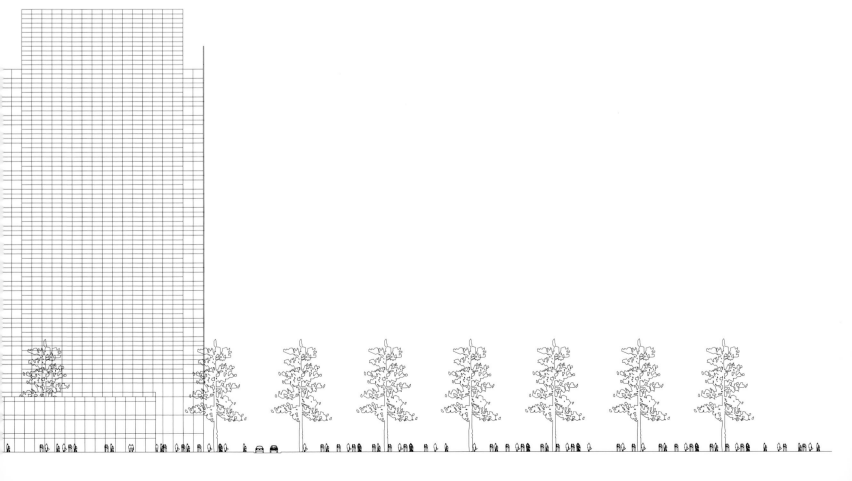

NEW INSTITUTIONS
BENENDEN HOSPITAL
MANCHESTER METROPOLITAN UNIVERSITY
UNIVERSITY OF SOUTHAMPTON
DE LA SALLE SCHOOL
SURE START LAVENDER NURSERY

BENENDEN HOSPITAL
KENT 1999–2002

listed Lister Wing, completed in
1937 and designed by Burnet,
Tait & Lorne in a progressive
manner influenced by both
Johannes Duiker's famous
Zonnestraal Sanatorium at
Hilversum and by the De La Warr
Pavilion at nearby Bexhill-on-Sea.
Indeed, Thomas Tait, the architect
of the Lister Wing, was chair of
the jury that selected Mendelsohn
and Chermayeff's project for the
Bexhill Pavilion (itself the subject
of an ongoing remodelling project
by McAslan; see p. 90).

The new clinic – which is a
research, as well as a treatment,
facility – replaces the Williams
Wing, an uninspired and badly
constructed near-replica of the
Lister Wing, built in the 1950s.
The construction of the Williams
Wing at that time involved the
demolition of the western 'bullnose'
end of the Lister Wing to form a
new link block between the two.
McAslan's brief was for a mix of
consulting rooms and procedure
rooms for minor operations,
plus waiting and support spaces,
for the treatment of in- and out-
patients.

The site for the new building
mirrored, almost exactly, that of
the Williams Wing, but there was
initially an expectation on the
part of planners that the new
block would complement, without
copying, the listed Tait building
and also repair damage done to
the latter in the 1950s. The lost
western end was, in fact,
reconstructed as part of the
project, with the remarkably thin
concrete roof slab extended under
the advice of Arup's engineers
and the original steel windows
reproduced.

The new link block is designed
in a deliberately neutral manner,
simply rendered and well set back
from both old and new buildings.
John McAslan + Partners' new
clinic is constructed on a steel
frame with floors formed on
concrete planks. The plan places
consulting rooms along the
southern edge at first-floor level,
where they benefit from the
splendid view, with a central
corridor flanked on the opposite
side by waiting rooms, WCs and
other patient facilities. The
procedure rooms are accessed
by medical staff via a corridor
along the northern edge of the
building, with a connection directly

Below
The new clinic at Benenden,
replacing a failed building of
the 1950s, adjoins the 1937
Lister Wing, a listed building to
which it defers in scale but not
in style.

Opposite
Facing south, the new building
is protected from direct sunlight
by a wall of fixed louvres.

The context for John McAslan +
Partners' new clinic at Benenden
Hospital, in the Weald of Kent, is
significant both in landscape and
architectural terms. The hospital
was established in 1906 to
accommodate "lower salaried
tubercular cases" (it is still run
by an independent trust) on a
spectacularly elevated site with
fine views and fresh air. Its
building stock is extremely varied
but includes the stylish, Grade II

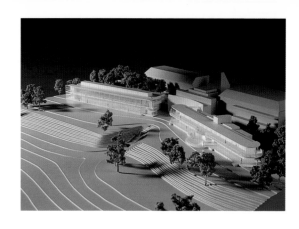

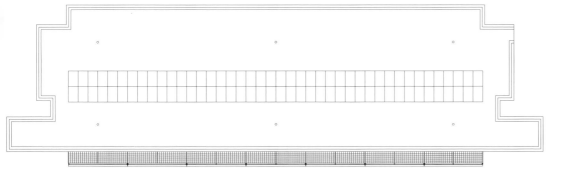

Below and opposite
Internal views of the south
corridor, procedure rooms, and
north corridor on the first floor.

Overleaf
To the south, the new
extension looks out over
the Weald of Kent.

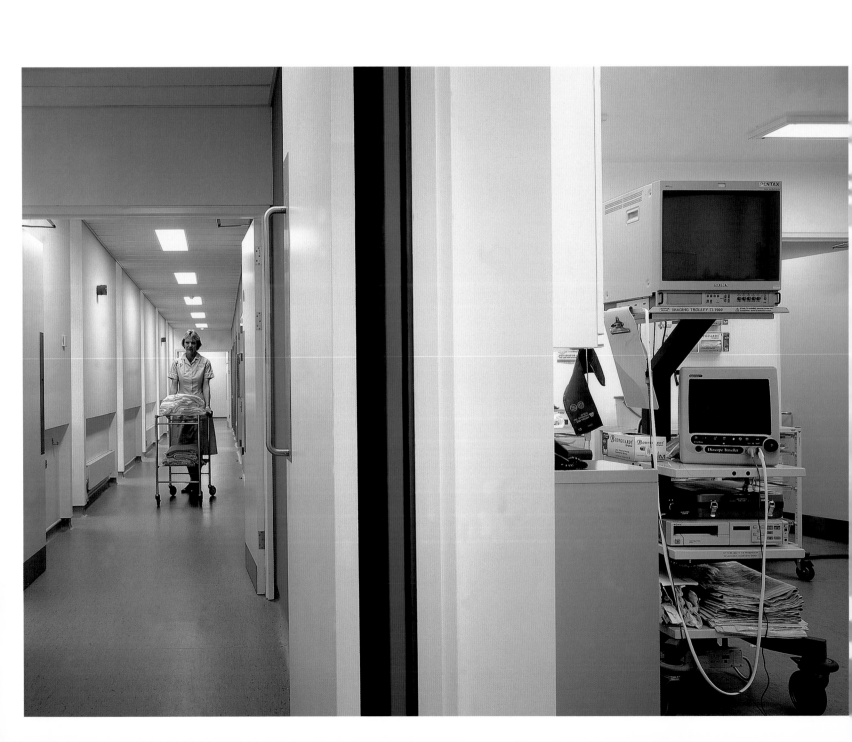

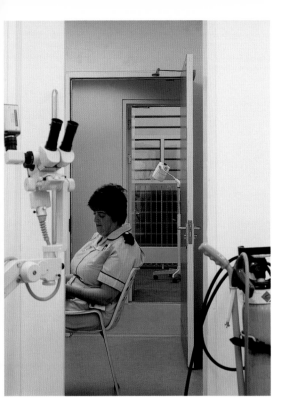

into the main hospital complex. Much of the ground floor is dedicated to sterile space used for the storage and preparation of surgical instruments and other material. Access stairs are provided at each end of the building in fully glazed enclosures – a reference back to the 'bullnoses' of the Tait building. The clinic is mostly served by natural ventilation, and servicing requirements are moderate so that ceiling voids could be utilized for plant.

While medical opinion in the 1930s counselled the exposure of TB patients to fresh air and sunshine (the Lister Wing has balconies facing south), the new clinic is protected against solar gain on its southern elevation by a wall of fixed louvres standing proud of the façade. The motivation for this device is practical but it has advantages in visual and architectural terms, giving the new building a layered appearance while allowing the new wing to emerge clearly as a lightweight pavilion in the landscape. On a limited budget, which did not allow for costly internal finishes, John McAslan + Partners produced a rigorous and elegant pavilion that complements its listed neighbour without deferring to it needlessly – indeed, the new building is anything but deferential. The project is an exercise in continuity and vigorous contextualism.

MANCHESTER METROPOLITAN UNIVERSITY
LAW FACULTY
MANCHESTER 2000–2003

Below and opposite
The context for the new Law Faculty at Manchester Metropolitan University is a 1960s and 1970s campus, tightly constrained to one side by an urban motorway.

Manchester Metropolitan University (MMU) is the UK's largest higher education institution, with over 32,000 students at present and a planned expansion to over 40,000. Granted university status in 1992, it occupies seven sites in the North-West of England, five of them in Manchester itself. The heart of MMU is the former Manchester Polytechnic campus at All Saints, off Manchester's Oxford Road and close to the campuses of the University of Manchester, UMIST (University of Manchester Institute of Science and Technology) and the Royal Northern College of Music.

The All Saints site extends along three sides of Grosvenor Square, formerly the churchyard of the demolished church of All Saints, and includes the historic premises of the former School of Art on the south side. The buildings on the north side were developed from 1971 onwards to designs by Sheppard Robson (the All Saints Building) and the City Architect's Department (the eleven-storey Loxford Building, now scheduled for redevelopment). John McAslan + Partners' Law Faculty (for which Matthew Burl was project architect) is part of a projected programme of renewal of the All Saints campus extending over more than a decade.

Initially, partial demolition of the All Saints Building was considered as part of the project, allowing accommodation for other departments to be provided, but this was subsequently rejected on cost grounds. The new law faculty is slotted into a 35 m × 25 m (115 ft × 82 ft) site behind the library wing of this block; the urban motorway of the Mancunian Way runs to the north (a hugely intrusive presence that bisects the MMU central campus), and the Loxford Building closely abuts it to the west.

The brief for the project, which John McAslan + Partners won in competitive interview in July 2000, was extremely demanding: a budget of under £10 million for a building of 5500 sq m (59,000 sq ft) and an expectation that the new faculty would be in use for the autumn term of 2003. The contract period was just fifty-five weeks. Such provisions would be commonplace in the field of commercial development, and their application to a higher education project reflects the pressure for expansion and value-for-money emanating from government.

The practice's response has been to produce a building that is not only highly practical, delivered on time and achieved within the budget, but is also a stylish addition to the rapidly changing fabric of central Manchester. It contains seven

levels of accommodation, mostly cellular offices for staff and seminar rooms but also including three larger lecture theatres and a ground-floor social space at the base of the galleria. From All Saints, the building emerges above the brick-clad mass of Sheppard Robson's earlier complex. From the Mancunian Way, it presents dramatic sight, its transparent glazed façade a striking contrast to the heaviness of earlier buildings in the vicinity. The motorway is, for the foreseeable future, a reality that

has to be confronted, and John McAslan has produced a building that does exactly that – advertising the dynamic presence of MMU to all who pass by. It is planned to create new pedestrian links below the road, connecting All Saints to the Faculty of Technology, which lies to the north.

Within the building, the noise of the Mancunian Way is perceived as no more than a reassuring murmur thanks to the acoustic engineering of the sealed glazed façade. The polluted context ruled out a natural ventilation solution – opening windows – but chilled beams have been used instead

as part of a low-energy mixed-mode cooling system. Where the building scores in energy terms is in its virtuoso use of controlled natural light, which makes artificial lighting superfluous in many areas in fine weather. At the heart of the block is a full-height day-lit atrium (only 3 m / 10 ft wide at its narrowest point, in fact) into which many of the offices have a view. Staircases, lifts and WCs are concentrated in a core along the east end of the building in the Kahnian mode that has become something of a hallmark of McAslan's architecture. A secondary core at the west end of the block contains an escape stair and will connect to a later phase

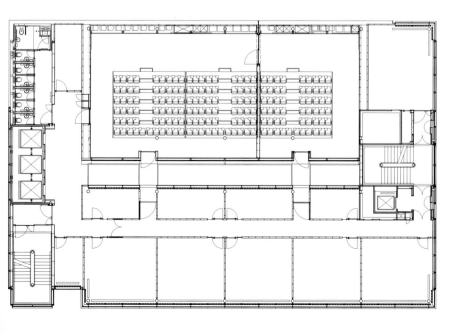

Above and below
The Law Faculty provides access to numerous work stations within a well-lit environment.

Opposite
From below, the curving hull of the lecture theatres falls away to create a generous public space.

Overleaf
From across the Mancunian Way, the stacked floors of the Law Faculty provide a luminous presence in the city.

of development. The main lecture theatres are accommodated in two double-height spaces along the south side of the building – two multi-purpose spaces (120 and 60 seats respectively, with bleacher seating) sit on top of a raked 240-seat auditorium. The theatre complex reads as a sculptural, curved, boat-like intervention into the atrium and is clad in strips of ash, which is also used internally as part of the acoustic formula. Glass bridges provide connections across the atrium to the upper theatre spaces and the top levels of the main auditorium. Casual seating (in the form of a 30 m / 100 ft long

bright yellow leather bean bag) is provided at ground level in the atrium, which doubles as a place of passage and social space.

In some senses, the building is, inevitably, introspective, something of an oasis in the city centre. Yet it also has a role as an urban connector, unlocking the barrier that cuts the campus in two. Achieving this, as well as meeting the practical demands of the brief, is part of the considerable success of this project.

UNIVERSITY OF SOUTHAMPTON ENGINEERING BUILDING
SOUTHAMPTON 2003–2005

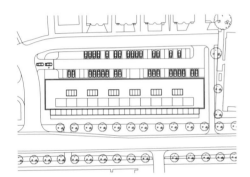

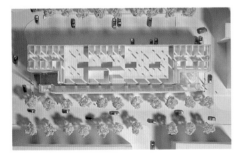

This project for a 7000 sq m (75,000 sq ft) block on Southampton University's Highfields campus reflects a major strand in John McAslan + Partners' work: the quest for a highly rational, flexible and deliverable design strategy that draws on the practice's experience of the commercial development world in the context of the special needs of the education sector. The scheme (like the law faculty at Manchester Metropolitan University, see p. 162) is a response to the demand from higher education institutions for high-value signature buildings that can be procured at an affordable price and to a rapid schedule.

The site is on a suburban campus, mainly low-rise and characterized by free-standing buildings in rolling green spaces. Earlier buildings there include several designed by the practice of Sir Basil Spence. More recently, a masterplan by Rick Mather has applied a new discipline to the development. John McAslan + Partners' site is on University Road, a broad thoroughfare that bisects the campus, for which it is the main point of entry. The brief was for a building that would house roughly half of the university's school of electronic and computer sciences, plus a new 'gateway' reception point for the campus, including a 360-seat lecture theatre and display area shared by all departments, together with a security centre. All this was to be achieved for not more than £10 million. The building (for which Alasdair Travers was McAslan's project architect) was seen as making a 'statement' about the identity of the university – a place where public, staff and students would interact.

The long, thin site (measuring 90 m × 15 m / 295 ft × 50 ft) determined the form of the building, which is essentially linear. In the layout eventually selected for development, the lecture theatre is integrated within the box of the four-storey building. Service cores form 'bookends' at each end. Circulation at all levels is via an internal galleria along the western edge of the block; voids provide a visual link between floors but are also important as part of a low-energy ventilation strategy, while the galleria buffers the internal spaces from external noise and solar gain. The precast concrete floor structure also plays

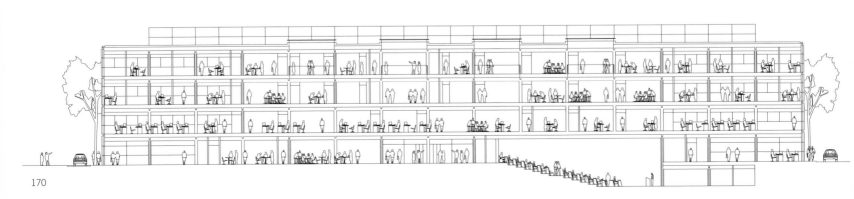

its part in the low-energy programme, providing thermal mass. Services are located in the exposed soffit. Perimeter offices along the eastern side of the building are naturally ventilated, though assisted ventilation is required in laboratory spaces. The western elevation is fitted with fixed louvres to baffle solar gain.

In plan, the building features public spaces, including the lecture theatre and its generous foyer area, at the southern end of the ground floor, with departmental accommodation to the north. The internal 'street' provides both a meeting place and a connection – this will be the 'front door' that the campus has hitherto lacked. The first floor is a highly flexible, largely open-plan teaching space for undergraduates. Second and third floors are principally intended for postgraduates and staff, and include areas of cellular offices. Light-wells provide a sense of connection between these upper levels.

This is a project where rigour and the discipline imposed by the structural grid, frankly expressed, are the determining factors. The development of the façade designs and particularly of the canopy marking the entrances at the north-west and south-west corners of the building will give it a clear identity and recognizable character.

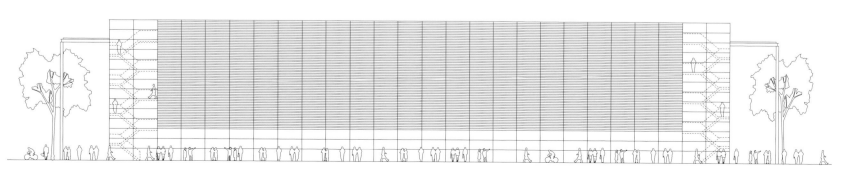

DE LA SALLE SCHOOL
MANCHESTER 2002–2004

Below and opposite
An addition to an existing school campus, the performing arts centre consists of linked pavilions with teaching and rehearsal rooms on two floors, the upper level being top-lit. On a small scale, the project exemplifies McAslan's use of a strong grid to define spaces and circulation routes.

Overleaf
The architectural forms and the palette of materials selected for the project are in tune with the rigour of the plan.

The performing arts centre at De La Salle School is a relatively modest building, in terms of both scale (750 sq m / 8000 sq ft gross) and cost (around £750,000), but it is seen as a significant 'landmark' addition to an institution that aspires to excellence in all its activities. The centre is also used by the wider community outside school hours. In common with a number of other educational projects by John McAslan + Partners, it features a strong and highly rational diagram, which provides extremely efficient internal spaces.

The centre is located south of the existing school complex – to which it physically connects – and adjacent to the main point of entry to the entire site, on land previously used for parking. Its proximity to neighbouring houses influenced the designs in a number of respects, not least in terms of acoustic insulation. The building consists of three linked pavilions, each containing flexible teaching/activity spaces for drama, music and dance at ground- and first-floor level. The ground-floor classrooms are glazed to the north and south and highly transparent, while the spaces on the first floor, double-height in form, are top-lit (the lanterns incorporate ventilation louvres) and heavily insulated to provide for maximum flexibility of use. The pavilions are separated by two staircases contained in glazed cores and connected by a ground-floor corridor – the first-floor spaces, which extend over the corridor, are larger in area than those at ground level. Two concrete towers on the south side of the building contain service spaces. A glazed reception area links the new building to the existing school complex.

The palette of materials is in tune with the rigour of the plan – fairfaced concrete, glass, timber and zinc cladding are used – and has been selected with a view to durability and resilience. This is a tough but humane building, designed for hard wear and to be enjoyed.

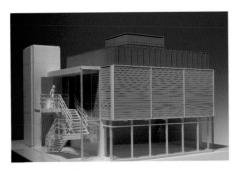

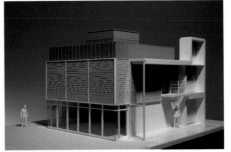

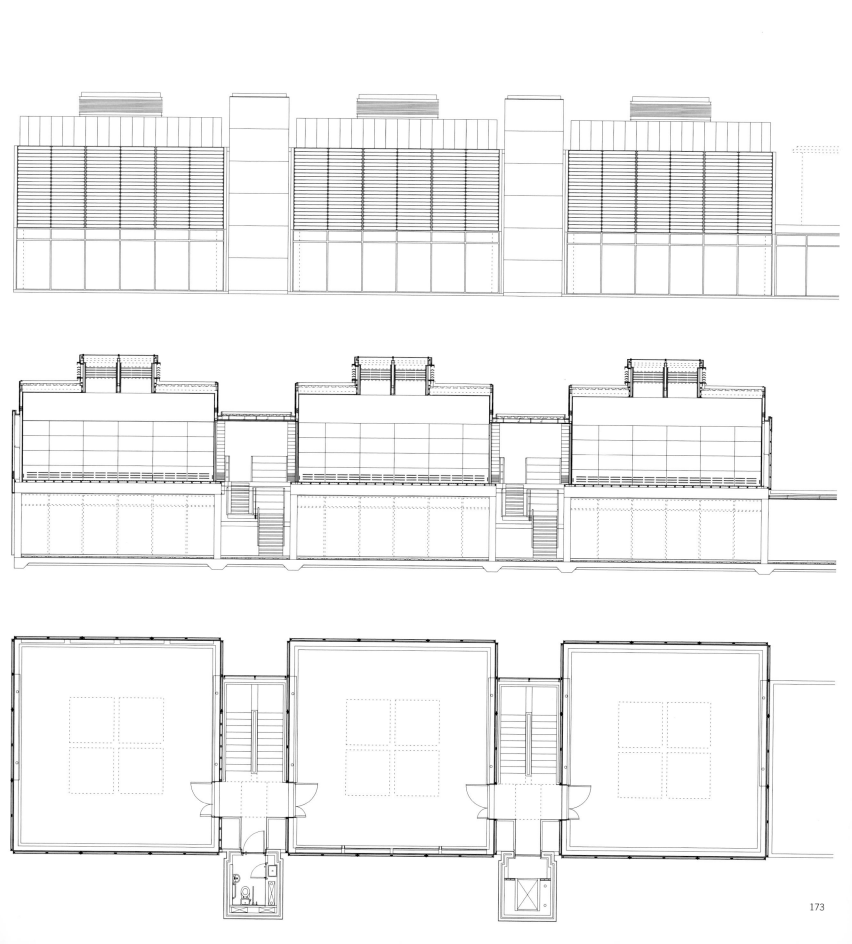

SURE START LAVENDER NURSERY
MITCHAM, LONDON 2002–2004

If one distinctive feature of John McAslan + Partners' work is the detailed process of research, experiment and design generated by its work on historic buildings and sites, another is the development of appropriate models for new buildings that offer high value, economy of means and flexibility for changing needs.

The Sure Start Lavender project epitomizes the latter strand in the practice's workload. The starting point was the UK Government's £500 million funding programme to provide nursery care and a framework of support and advice for low-income families – the social group that needs them

most. The brief in this instance was for a nursery that would accommodate seventy children and babies, plus community facilities including a café.

The site at Tamworth Park, Mitcham, in the south London borough of Merton, has an unfortunate history in that the pavilion that previously stood there was destroyed by fire in 2001. The site had subsequently been vacant, but is close to established leisure facilities and conveniently located within a residential area. The Sure Start project is much more than a nursery school: it aims to revitalize the surrounding park and to contribute to the regeneration of the whole neighbourhood.

Appointed early in 2003 following a design competition, John McAslan + Partners has developed the project with a view to completion in 2004 – rapid procurement was seen as vital. The new 1000 sq m (10,800 sq ft) building is conceived as a single-storey 'pavilion in the park', colourful and attractive but also highly practical. Economy in terms of capital cost (£1.4 million) is achieved by using standardized

components and modular construction – a kit-of-parts approach on a steel frame that recalls the classic British schools of the 1950s and 1960s – while low-energy design, notably the use of controlled natural light and natural ventilation, reduces running costs. In plan, the building forms a layered arrangement of services and support spaces facing the busy London Road, the activity rooms (plus the café) being expressed as a series of separate pavilions beyond and, to the rear, facing the park, secure open-air play spaces. The glazed elevations of the activity rooms are designed to open up to the play areas. To the street, the building has a more solid look with panels of

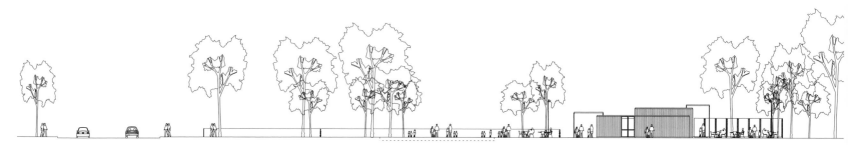

coloured glazing articulating the timber cladding. It would be all too easy for a building like this to assume a defensive look, but the aim instead is to make it a well-regarded community asset with a welcoming and friendly appearance.

In its overall conception, at least, Sure Start is part of a family of McAslan buildings that includes the extension to Benenden Hospital, the engineering block at Southampton University and, more recently, a new proposal for a City Academy in Croydon. Sure Start Lavender Nursery presents a model for a new community architecture that is worthy of its name, providing not only useful facilities but also an element of delight.

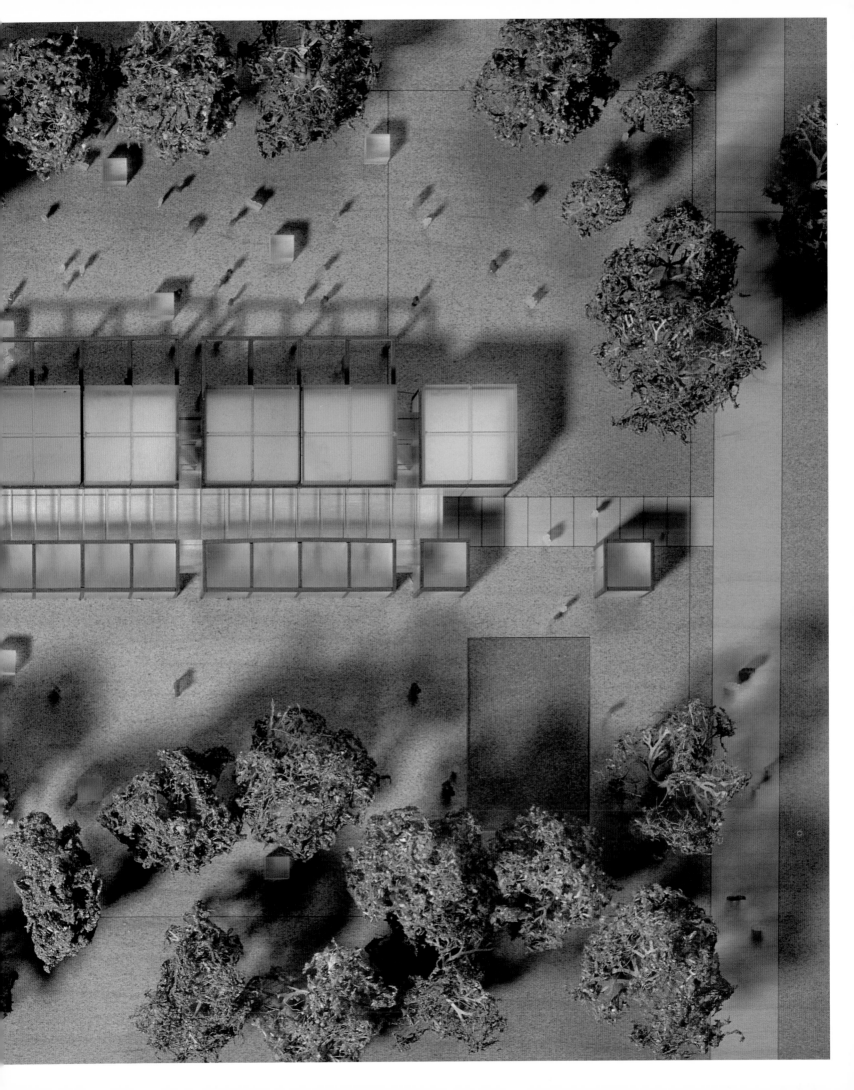

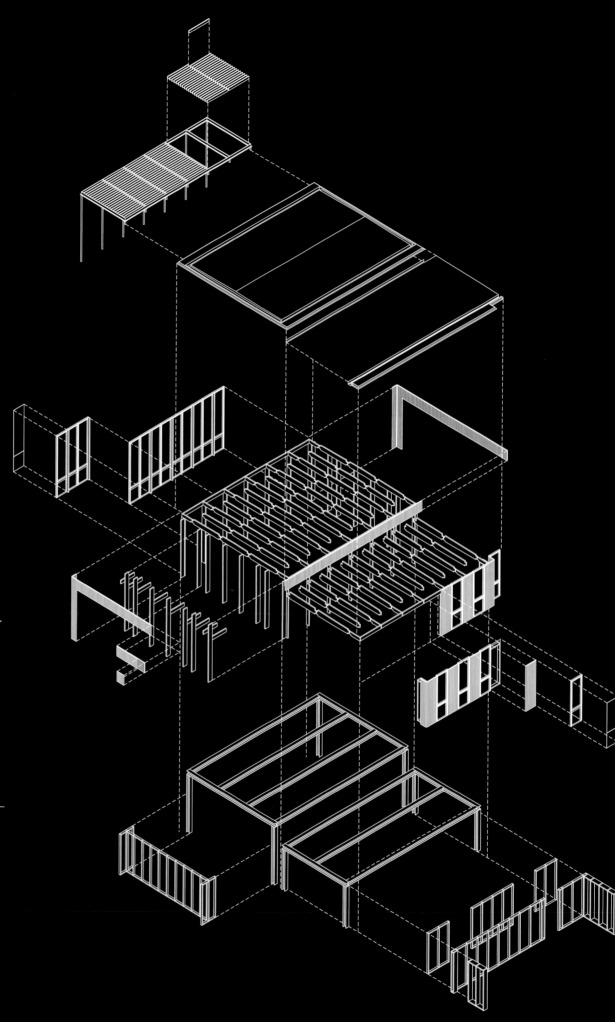

Modular Mathematics

There are many scientific and mathematical formulae that at first glance appear almost ludicrously simple, although in fact we know that the various terms – represented by letters or Greek symbols – are assembled in a very particular way. The purity of expression in these equations belies the complexity of thought involved in reaching a solution. The individual terms fit together to make a whole, which elegantly encapsulates the interdependencies of the variables to describe a singular truth. This truth may change or –

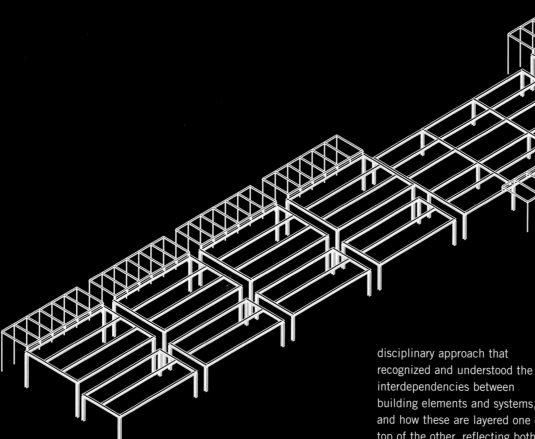

as in the case of Einstein's *E=mc²* – challenge our perception of the world around us.

This inspires a design approach to buildings where the final form seeks to be clean and simple, yet more than the sum of its parts – fulfilling its function and providing an opportunity to enhance the surroundings and change the perception of the buildings' users.

The users of the Sure Start Nursery project at Tamworth Park include 18 babies and 74 two- to four-year-olds. Pragmatism dictated that the building form should be simple, and the number of elements kept to

a minimum while being repeated as much as possible. Programming issues were minimized by limiting *in situ* construction. The building was thus conceived as a kit of parts that could be fabricated off-site, delivered on trucks and assembled in a matter of weeks. Essentially, it is a giant Lego or Meccano kit – in itself an appropriate concept and one that is legible to users.

The challenge was to achieve clarity and simplicity by developing and distilling down the design to a series of discrete elements that would fit perfectly together. This required an inter-

disciplinary approach that recognized and understood the interdependencies between building elements and systems, and how these are layered one on top of the other, reflecting both the order in which construction might take place and the interfaces between contractors.

Conceptually, building services, envelope and finishes were built up in layers anchored by the structural frame, in the same way that muscles, organs, skin and, finally, clothing flesh out a skeleton to define a person. All interconnect to create the overall appearance of the building.

Modular building implies quality pattern-cutting and tailoring rather than loose-fit construction, and the modular approach requires a particular design effort to refine the building into a coherent kit of parts. This form of construction is based on the idea of developing a prototype that might be repeated, even mass-produced. Potentially, the kit of parts can be adapted for other sites, even other uses, or it can simply be assembled in a slightly different way – just like Lego.

Jo da Silva

URBAN INFRASTRUCTURE
KING'S CROSS STATION
CROSSRAIL PADDINGTON STATION
PICCADILLY GARDENS INTERCHANGE
KELVIN LINK BRIDGE
ST GEORGE'S ISLAND
182–188 KENSINGTON CHURCH STREET

KING'S CROSS STATION
LONDON 1998–2009

Below
The new concourse at King's Cross Station is sited to the west of the 1850s terminus, in a pivotal location between the Channel Tunnel Rail Link terminal at St Pancras and the major new commercial and residential quarter on the former goods yard site to the north.

Opposite
The filigree diagrid roof of the new concourse extends to embrace a new public space between the two termini, while the removal of the ugly 1970s southern concourse allows a new square to be created to the south of King's Cross.

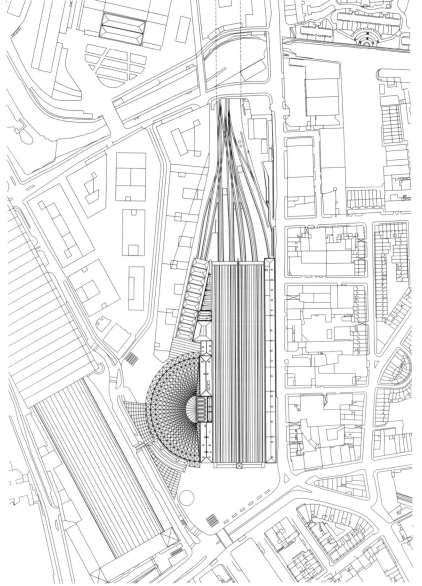

King's Cross Station, completed in 1852, is one of the great railway monuments of Britain, notable (especially in the context of its neighbour, the Gothic Revival St Pancras) for the restrained dignity of its twin train sheds, designed by Lewis Cubitt as the terminus of the Great Northern Railway. In the early years of the Modern Movement it was acclaimed for its 'functionalism'. Today, King's Cross is the London terminal for the East Coast mainline route from Scotland, North-East England and Yorkshire, and for commuter services from East Anglia and parts of the Home Counties. With its associated Thameslink and London Underground stations, the latter one of the busiest in the capital and currently undergoing reconstruction, King's Cross is one of the most intensively used transport interchanges in Europe, with up to fifty million passengers passing through annually. The impending arrival of the Channel Tunnel Rail Link (CTRL) at St Pancras and the long-awaited development of the neighbouring goods yard as a new commercial and residential district may have increased the pressure for improvements to the Grade I listed King's Cross Station, but the key factor is the need for a new multi-modal interchange at this vital transport node.

John McAslan + Partners was commissioned by Railtrack in 1998 to prepare a masterplan for the development of the station. It has since progressed the project for Railtrack's successor, Network Rail, following a commitment of support from the UK Government in 2002.

Passenger facilities at King's Cross have long been inadequate. Ticket offices and shops are housed in a 'temporary' southern extension of the 1970s, a structure of poor quality that the planning authority wishes to see replaced. With the arrival of the CTRL, the aim is to integrate King's Cross and St Pancras stations more effectively and to create a dynamic public realm around them. The stations are seen as engines of regeneration, contributing to the transformation of King's Cross, long seen as a seedy backwater, into an attractive area in which to live and work. In anticipation of this, the area east of the station (now known as Regent's Quarter) is already being redeveloped as a mixed-use, high-value urban neighbourhood, containing a mix of refurbishment and new build.

The key to the project is the removal of the ugly southern concourse and its replacement by a new western concourse facing St Pancras and sitting over the new Underground ticket hall. With its mesh of subterranean routes and services, this site poses challenging structural problems but its location facilitates interchange between the Underground and mainline stations – sixty per cent of rail users arrive at King's Cross by Underground. The great arched frontage of the station on Euston Road will re-emerge as a landmark and a conspicuous point of entry and exit. The area

between station and road (likely to remain a major thoroughfare for the foreseeable future) will be landscaped as a public square, which could perhaps be extended south of the road.

The new western concourse has been designed, in association with engineers Arup, as a strikingly sculptural glazed structure with a diagrid roof, a form that offers lightness and economy of means and neatly integrates the main roof span with the canopy extending into the adjacent public square. The concourse, which John McAslan modestly characterizes as "a piazza with an umbrella", will contain ticket offices, passenger lounges and retail/catering units with escalator links to the Underground. The listed train sheds are to be comprehensively refurbished, with some extension

of circulation space and a new platform created in the carriage road on the eastern edge of the station. The suburban platforms on the west side of the mainline terminus are to be retained and adapted, though the planned development of the Thameslink route will reduce pressure on them.

In terms of urban design, the project poses considerable challenges, notably in providing a 'gateway' to the regenerated goods yard – potentially the largest development zone in London. Taxis, buses and some through

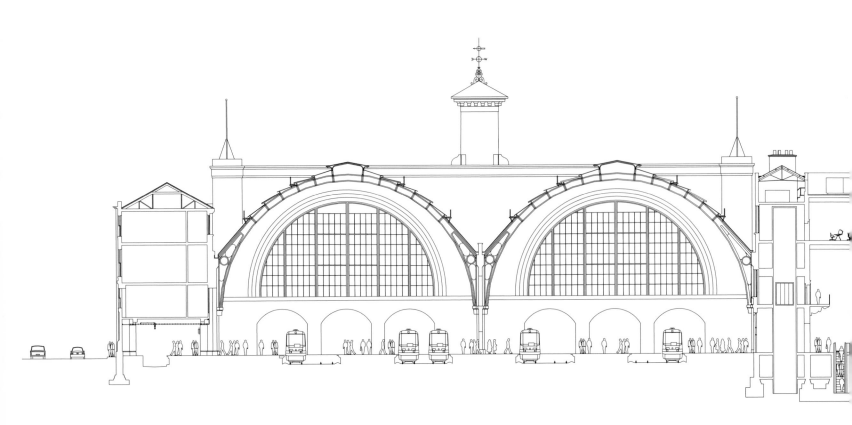

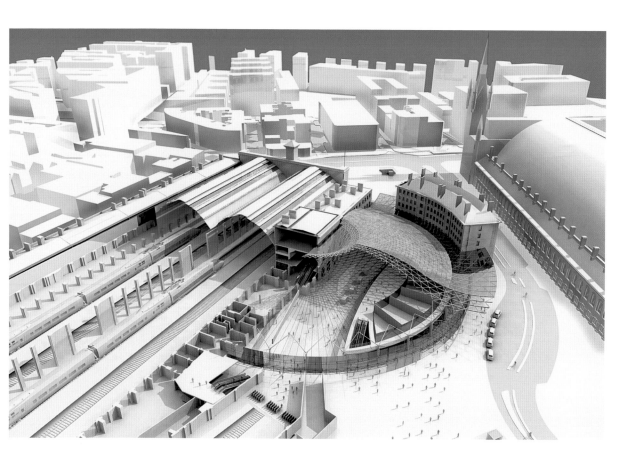

Opposite
In its elegance of form, the new passenger concourse is in the spirit of Victorian engineering, although the diagrid shell roof could only have been designed using modern computer technology.

Left and below
The new concourse roof sweeps down to embrace the piazza linking King's Cross and St Pancras stations, providing greatly improved connections to the Underground as well as much enhanced passenger amenities. The listed Great Northern Hotel is retained as part of the scheme and finally given the appropriate setting it has long lacked.

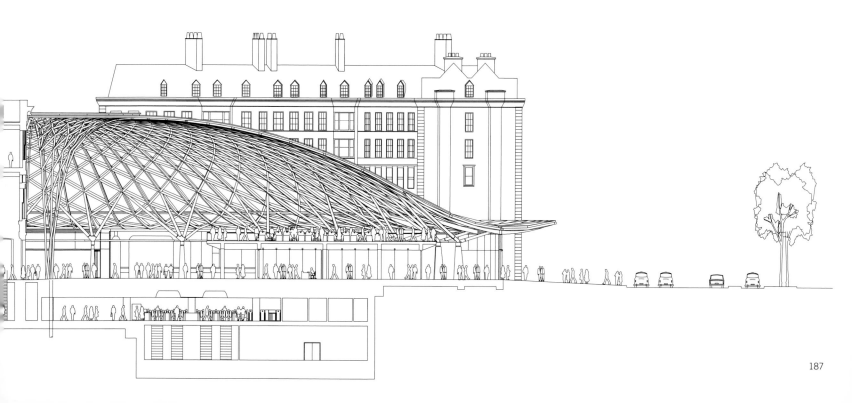

187

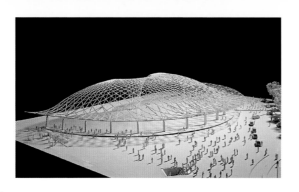

This page and opposite
The form of the roof, developed in conjunction with engineers at Arup, is a radical evolution of the railway architecture of the nineteenth century – light and ethereal in comparison with the massive timber, iron and glass roofs of the 1850s sheds.

Overleaf
The form of the roof expresses something of the dynamism of travel, while its structural efficiency provides a great public space unencumbered by columns.

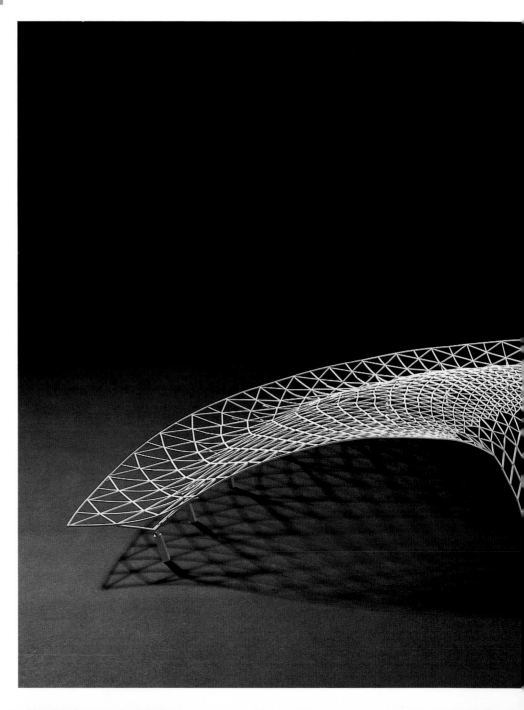

traffic have to be accommodated, and the issue of integrating surviving historic buildings addressed. These include the unique German Gymnasium and the Great Northern Hotel, a building that would intrude into the new public space between King's Cross and St Pancras and might beneficially be removed. If this could be achieved, the urban design intentions underlying the proposed new concourse, seen as a pivot between the two stations, could be more readily achieved.

The King's Cross project has been a highly demanding one for the McAslan team, headed by Adam Brown as project director. It has drawn on all aspects of the practice's expertise in the repair and reuse of historic buildings, in urban and landscape design, and in the creation of bold and innovative new structures – all within the context of an area with a complex pattern of use and ownership and where immense constraints are imposed by the existence of subterranean services. The £275 million project is now being developed with a view to a start on site in 2005 and completion in 2009.

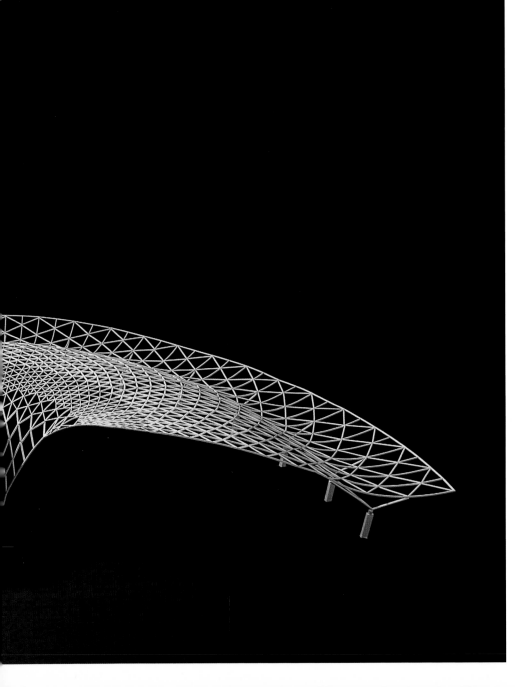

Form Finding

As we pass St Pancras Station going east on the Euston Road the darkness gathers and we enter the complications of King's Cross. The streets are mean and the buildings faceless, the twin arches of the station entrance lost in the urban congestion. Nothing is clear – where are we going?

A new plan illuminates. A triangular plaza borders Pancras Road and the Euston Road,

and on its largest oblique the façade of the original station is celebrated again. But this is just a signal, a past emblem: the real entrance is now along Pancras Road, a huge disc of a structure along the side of the station radiating out to welcome the visitor. A massive eye opens over the complex interchange: passengers, trains, mysterious interconnections, escalators cascading down into underground tunnels – all lie beneath and beyond. The rim of the structure

orbits low, drawing in the visitor. In section, the roof is a parabolic trajectory that flares out on all sides only to be pulled down again into the central focus, a patterned screen that meets the ground, heralding the entrance into the station. A structure of thin steel weaves intricate three-way patterns over the vault, one direction running towards the entrance, the other two spiralling diagonally, pulling against the line of that first indicator. The result is a retina of diamond

cells, capable of opacity, transparency, and a widening and narrowing horizon as the curvature changes from outer rim into plunging interior funnel. As the roof converges, the pattern closes and slips down like a mantle to the station entrance, which also serves as a trellis column. A veiled threat or playful welcome?

Cecil Balmond

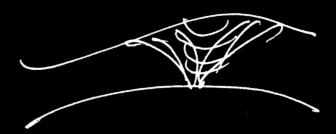

Below and opposite
The Crossrail station at Paddington is located in a great slice through the ground extending the whole length of Eastbourne Terrace, west of the Grade I listed station.

The Crossrail project was conceived more than a decade ago but only received a formal go-ahead from central government in 2003, although in early 2004 funding for its construction was still to be identified. Crossrail creates, in essence, an east–west rail link across central London (from Paddington to Liverpool Street and into the Isle of Dogs, with a direct link from Canary Wharf to Heathrow). A series of major stations is planned in central London. At Paddington, where John McAslan + Partners was appointed in 2003, the last decade has seen the commence-ment of major residential and commercial developments in the former goods yard and around the canal basin east of the mainline station. A major refurbishment and extension scheme for the latter is in progress. By 2016 passenger movements at Paddington are expected to increase by twenty-five per cent, though Crossrail will relieve the pressure on existing platform provision.

Crossrail, like the RER in Paris, is a mainline railway running below ground but at a depth more comparable to the Underground's Circle and Metropolitan lines than the deeper Tube routes. This has several advantages – relatively easy

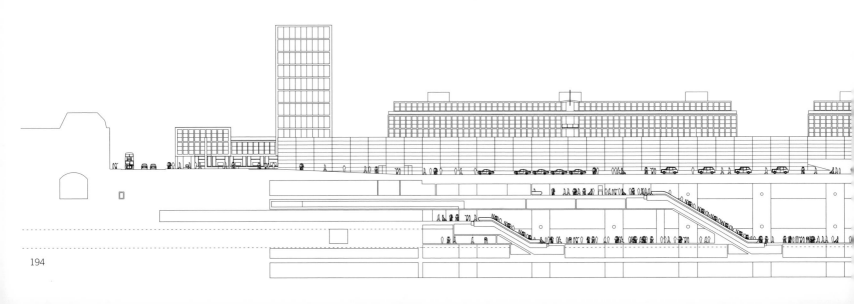

connections to both the mainline station and the Underground, for example, and the potential to use some daylight at platform level. In this respect, the project develops ideas seen in some of the Jubilee Line Extension stations constructed during the later 1990s.

The Crossrail station is located below Eastbourne Terrace and adjacent to the mainline station

designed by Isambard Kingdom Brunel. The future configuration of this street remains to be resolved in line with the local authority's strategy for traffic management in the Paddington area. The station is envisaged as an incision into the ground running the length of Eastbourne Terrace and creating a vast subterranean space. In form it is far removed from the typical London Underground station, with its separated tunnels, and more akin to Norman Foster's metro stations in Bilbao or the same architect's Jubilee Line station at Canary Wharf. The

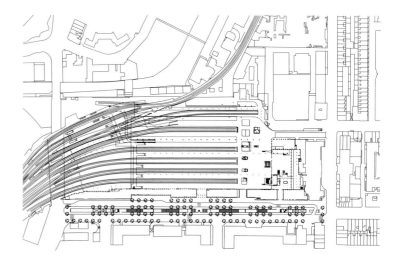

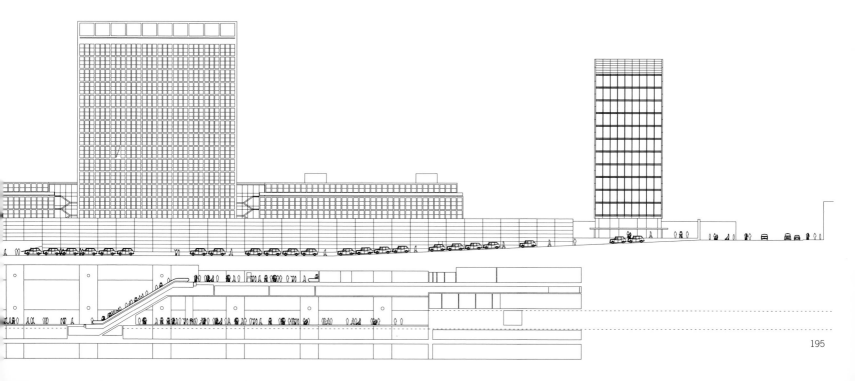

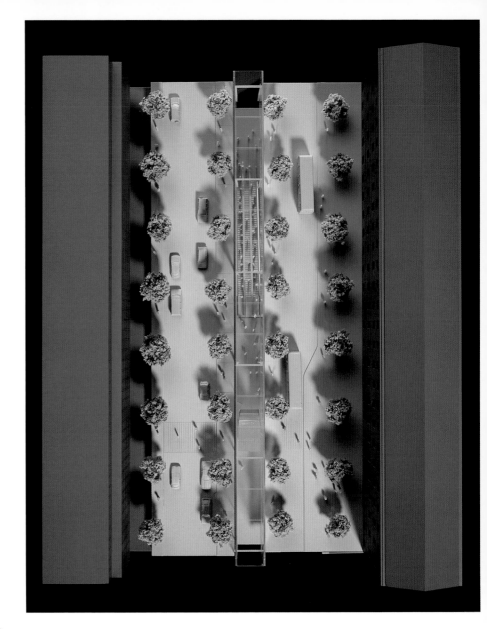

This page and opposite
The new station is externally
expressed as a glazed pavilion,
transparent and inviting,
rationalizing the approach to
Brunel's terminus.

station will be day-lit with a 300 m (980 ft) long glazed pavilion providing a dramatic marker at street level, and escalators descending from booking hall to platforms. Both above and below ground, the architecture aims to orientate and to rationalize the movement of people and vehicles in what is presently a rather confused scene.

One aspiration of the scheme is to provide a new western entrance to Brunel's station, essentially an internalized structure that has always suffered from its siting in a cutting (below the level of the surrounding streets and nearby canal) and has never had a clearly discernible point of entry. A generous piazza could be formed between the Crossrail station and the long side elevation of the Brunel station, with the war-damaged sections of the latter finally reconstructed. The new station will be a twenty-first century work of architecture and engineering worthy of its location.

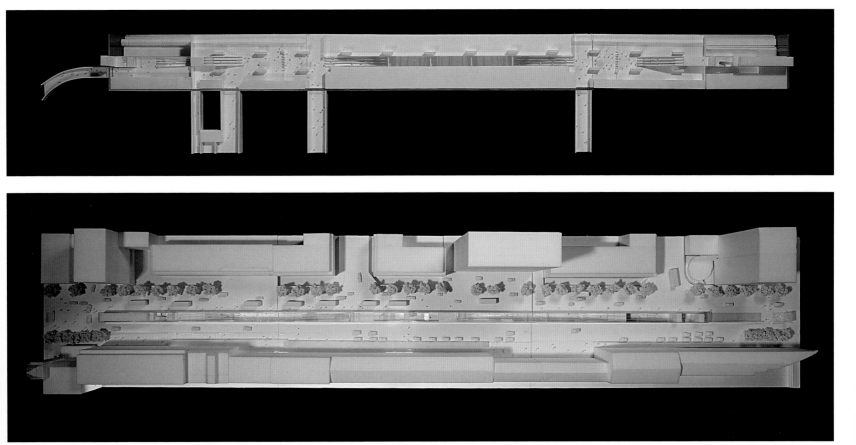

PICCADILLY GARDENS INTERCHANGE
MANCHESTER 2003–2005

Below
The canopies covering the new bus station at Piccadilly Gardens, Manchester, are clad in lightweight ETFE cushions, which form umbrellas to protect passengers from the weather while avoiding a needless sense of enclosure.

Opposite
The project forms part of a comprehensive reconstruction of the surrounding area, which includes Tadao Ando's distinctive concrete pavilion structure as well as the interchange for the city's tram system.

Piccadilly Gardens is arguably, more than Albert Square, the true heart of Manchester. It was created as a public space early in the twentieth century when the old Royal Infirmary that stood there was demolished and relocated. Its proximity to the city's main retail quarter and to Piccadilly Station make it a natural focus, though in recent years the gardens assumed a rundown appearance. Tadao Ando's new pavilion, standing within a newly landscaped square, has restored something of the dignity of the site, although the massive 1960s Piccadilly Plaza development provides a rather overbearing backdrop.

The arrival of the city's tram system has reinforced the importance of Piccadilly Gardens as a transport interchange. John McAslan + Partners was recently commissioned to prepare proposals for a replacement bus station to extend between the new square and Piccadilly Plaza (the facility is currently very inadequate). The aim was to avoid the typical all-over canopy, which tends to make bus stations into oppressive, poor-quality enclosed environments, but at the same time provide protection from the unpredictable Manchester weather by inserting new elements with a more human scale. The bus station has to remain in use throughout the project and so a sequential approach was needed.

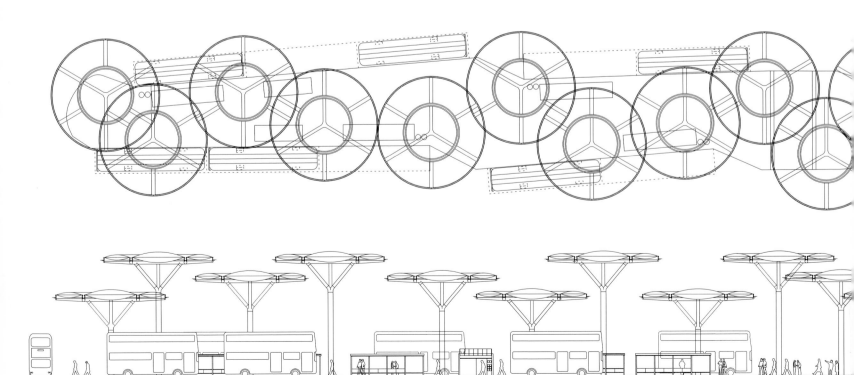

Overleaf
The informal geometry and lightweight appearance of the canopies contrasts strongly with the adjacent 1960s buildings.

A modular solution has been proposed, with ETFE cushions forming lightweight 'petals' or umbrellas – individual freestanding elements – supported on steel columns. The ETFE (recently successfully used in the reconstruction of Piccadilly Station) allows natural light to flow through during daylight hours, while at night it provides a luminous surface at which artificial light can be directed. The arrangement of these circular, interlocking canopies has an informality that responds specifically to the operational layout of the bus station while also giving it a clear identity. The elegance of the canopies is intended to complement the overall renewal of the surrounding quarter of the city and to provide a proper degree of dignity and comfort for the bus traveller.

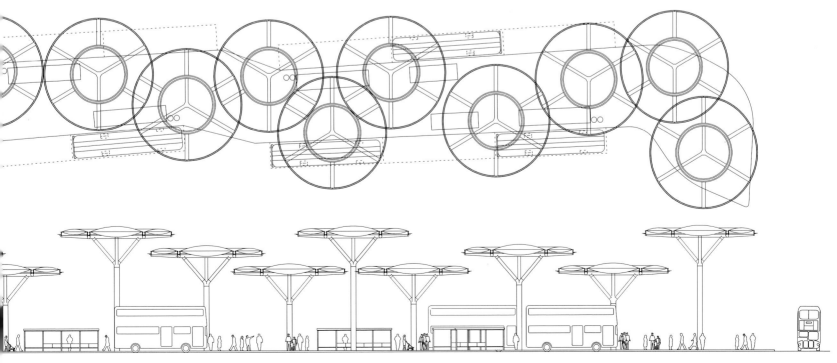

KELVIN LINK BRIDGE
GLASGOW 1999—2005

Bridges are essentially functional structures, but they can also be beautiful. In recent years architects have increasingly worked with engineers to bridge voids in ways that can be memorable, even inspirational. John McAslan + Partners' collaboration with Anthony Hunt Associates on the Kelvin Link Bridge project is an excellent example. The objective was, however, not simply to produce a visually striking bridge, offering an exciting response to a practical

brief, but, more significantly, to infuse the surrounding historic landscape with a new sense of drama and spectacle.

The site for the bridge is Glasgow's Kelvingrove Park, originally a private domain but acquired by the city in 1852 and laid out as a place of public recreation under the influence of Sir Joseph Paxton (of Crystal Palace fame). Between 1888 and 1911 the park was the location of three great international exhibitions that asserted the place of Glasgow as the second city of the British Empire. The 'aerial railway' constructed across the Kelvin valley for the 1911 exhibition was perhaps the most spectacular feature of any of these events, which were hugely popular in their time and still resonate today. Images of the aerial structure fired the imagination of the McAslan/Hunt design team as they developed a submission for the 1999 open competition for a bridge across the valley.

The occasion for the project was the 550th anniversary of the University of Glasgow, which relocated from the industrialized east of the city to Gilmorehill in the fashionable West End in the later nineteenth century. The university's main building, designed by Sir Giles Gilbert Scott, is one of the landmarks of Glasgow, balanced on the other side of the valley by the flamboyant bulk of the Kelvingrove Museum and Art

Gallery, which opened in 1901. The bridge is designed to connect the two great institutions – which are just 250 m (800 ft) apart but separated by a level change of 25 m (80 ft) across the steep valley. But it is not just institutions that will be linked. The bridge is set to transform perceptions of this quarter of the city and perhaps even revive some of the heady emotions that the were kindled by the great exhibitions of the past.

Project director Murray Smith describes the competition-winning scheme as "a sinuous route through trees, winding from ground level to canopy and back again". He adds: "The essence of the Kelvin Link is a fluid engagement with Kelvingrove, intensifying the dynamic

Opposite and this page
The link is really two bridges,
at high and low level, touching
and forming new pedestrian
routes through Kelvingrove Park.

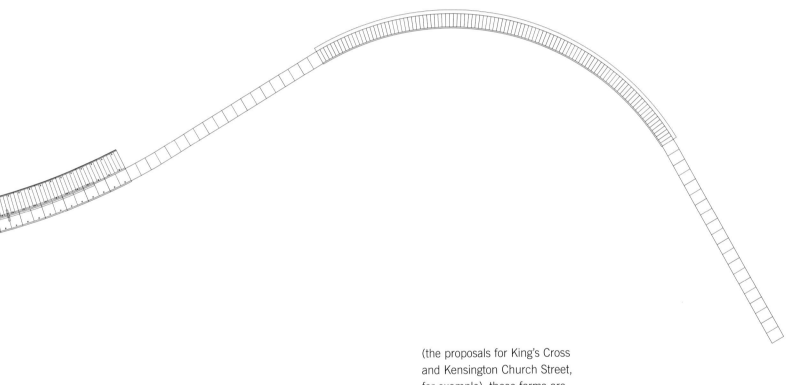

(the proposals for King's Cross
and Kensington Church Street,
for example), these forms are
informed by practical as much as
aesthetic aspirations.

The bridge, in fact, provides
two distinct connections – linking
university to gallery at high level
and, below, forming a new link in
the existing system of riverside
pathways around the park. The
two curving routes meet mid-span,
around 12 m (40 ft) above the
river, providing a new point of
meeting and orientation for the
site. The primary walkway is 120
m (400 ft) long, a lightweight steel

experiences of the park and
drawing its existing network of
pathways towards a new focal
point above the river Kelvin."
Making use of sophisticated CAD
modelling, the scheme reflects
John McAslan + Partners'
increasing interest in highly
expressive and dynamic forms.
As elsewhere in McAslan's work

structure with a deck of precast
concrete supported on V-columns,
and the bridge is perceived as
a detached plane sweeping
through the trees. There are no
masts or cables to compromise
this image. An art installation
by Ron Haselden is designed to
illuminate the bridge by night,
using air movement to produce
colour effects that respond to
the seasons and the changing
Glasgow weather.

Below and opposite
The St George's Island development occupies a narrow site, long derelict and squeezed between canal and railway, and provides a dense and high-quality mixed-use environment close to the centre of Manchester.

St George's Island – it is islanded on one side by the Bridgewater Canal, on the other by a Victorian railway viaduct that today carries metro trains – lies on the edge of Manchester city centre, just beyond the rejuvenated Castlefield quarter. (The island takes its name from the nearby Regency church of St George, now converted into apartments.) The surrounding area is rapidly being regenerated with new housing, much of it in converted warehouses though a new apartment block is a local

landmark. Manchester has an outstanding record in reviving the idea of city-centre living.

Working for locally based developer Dandara, John McAslan + Partners has produced a masterplan and design for a substantial high-density residential and commercial development on the 1 ha (2.5 acre) site which, though long derelict, has a strong historical resonance. The Bridgewater Canal, opened in 1761, was Britain's first working canal and was a major catalyst for the growth of industry and commerce in Manchester. The St George's Island site was occupied from 1850 by an ironworks; this closed in 1911 and was finally cleared away in the 1960s, the land being subsequently developed as a bus depot. It is the historic significance of the area, rather than its scenic appeal, that led to its inclusion within a conservation area.

The development of the project had to address complex issues of ownership, access, ground contamination and noise, as well as the ongoing deterioration of the canalside, where the canal edge was crumbling. An appropriate

overall design strategy for the site had to be developed and various options were explored, including the possibility of a single linear block of housing along the canal. The view of John McAslan + Partners, however, was that the scale and nature of the site needed a thoroughly urban approach, with the creation of attractive communal space around the buildings. It was also seen as important that the residential blocks should sit at ground level (rather than on a podium) and enjoy a direct relationship with the canalside.

The scheme now provides for 330 apartments, in a range of sizes and plan types, in five

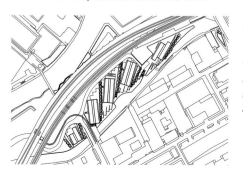

buildings ranging in height from seven to eleven storeys (the latter at the north-eastern tip of the site). The radial layout of the blocks was designed to provide optimum views without compromising privacy, and responds to the context of the site as defined by the canal and railway. In practical terms, it allows daylight to penetrate the apartments and limits the degree to which they are overlooked, but this is also a dynamic piece of urbanism, producing a fluid spatial composition and in particular addressing the monumentality of the nearby viaduct. Parking is located in two levels of basements. The landscape strategy for the site distinguishes between the canalside itself, where finishes are appropriately hard in an industrial mould, and the private gardens beyond, where planting provides a softer environment as an oasis from the city. Being developed to utilize modular construction techniques, this is a scheme that creates its own context in a rapidly changing urban landscape dominated by historic infrastructure.

Construction of the scheme will be phased, with a view to completion during 2007.

Opposite and this page
The form of the development responds to the site's constraints in order to maximize daylight and views.

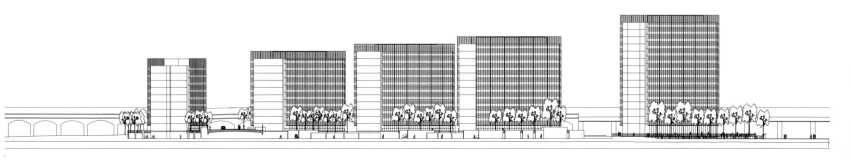

interest in strong form evident in McAslan's recent work. Inherent to this project is an ambition to produce architecture that, though essentially practical and rational, has the potential to surprise and challenge.

The site is bounded on one side by Kensington Church Street and on the other by Rabbit Row, a back street that is actually heavily used as a pedestrian short cut towards Kensington Gardens. An important element of the scheme is the provision of much-improved connections between the two streets, with a rejuvenated public realm animated by shops and cafés. The McAslan team, led by Murray Smith, worked with Cecil Balmond of Arup on the development of the project. The aim was to produce a practical and buildable proposal that both looked good and provided high-quality retail and residential space.

In order to produce a street level clear of obstructions, the development is designed to touch the ground at only three points.

Large, irregularly shaped floors are kept free of internal support: the structure is in the skin. The form of the scheme also defers to established rights of light, though the new building breaks the regular line of adjacent parapets. Produced using advanced CAD technology, this project, which has the support of Kensington & Chelsea planners, actually maximizes the amount of usable space that can be obtained on the site, opening up an otherwise inaccessible footprint. At John McAslan + Partners there is a growing willingness to explore form-making, not in an arbitrary way but with clearly defined objectives, in order to produce buildings that are both practical and aesthetically highly charged.

Below and opposite
The fluid form of the development at Kensington Church Street is certainly visually striking but is far from arbitrary. At ground level, the scheme unlocks the heart of the site and provides new connections across this space for pedestrians.

This mixed-use development occupies a site close to John McAslan + Partners' former offices near Notting Hill Gate and just outside the Kensington Church Street conservation area. The project gives Notting Hill Gate – a well-known address but also notable for the poor-quality redevelopment that took place there in the 1960s – a striking gateway and reflects the growing

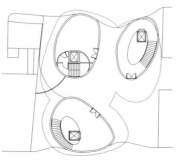

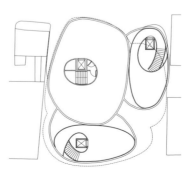

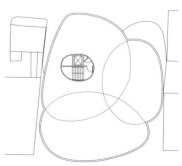

PROJECT CREDITS

Volubilis Site Museum

Client
Royaume du Maroc, Ministère des Affaires Culturelles
Team
John McAslan + Partners (Architect)
Arup (Multi-disciplinary Engineer)
University College London (Archaeologist)
L'Institut National des Sciences de l'Archéologie et du Patrimoine (Archaeologist)
Area
n/a
Value
£5 million / EUR 8 million
Programme
1998–2006

Royal Academy of Music

Client
Royal Academy of Music
Team
John McAslan + Partners (Architect)
Davis Langdon Management (Project Manager)
Oscar Faber (Multi-disciplinary Engineer)
Gardiner & Theobald (Cost Consultant)
Ralph Appelbaum Associates (Museum Design Consultant)
Sandy Brown Associates (Acoustics Consultant)
David Bonnett (Access Consultant)
Simons Interiors London (Contractor)
Area
3000 sq m / 32,000 sq ft
Value
£6 million / EUR 9 million
Programme
1997–2005

Trinity College of Music

Client
Trinity College of Music
Team
John McAslan + Partners (Architect)
Arup (Multi-disciplinary Engineer)
Arup Acoustics (Acoustic Engineer)
Davis, Langdon & Everest (Cost Consultant)
Healey and Baker (Development Consultant)
Purcell Miller Tritton (Historic Building Consultant)
Wates (Contractor)
Area
7500 sq m / 81,000 sq ft
Value
£5 million / EUR 8 million
Programme
1999–2002

Sugar Warehouse

Client
The Phoenix Trust
Project Clydeport plc (Peel Holdings)
Scottish Enterprise, Renfrewshire
Inverclyde Council
Team
John McAslan + Partners (Architect)
Arup Scotland (Multi-disciplinary Engineer)
Davis, Langdon & Everest (Cost Consultant)
DTZ Pieda Consulting (Development Appraisal Consultant)
ARP Lorimer & Associates (Historic Building Consultant)
Area
20,000 sq m / 215,000 sq ft
Value
n/a
Programme
2003–2008

Roundhouse

Client
Norman Trust
Team
John McAslan + Partners
(Architect)
Anthony Hunt Associates
(Structural Engineer)
Buro Happold
(Services Engineer)
Paul Gillieron
(Acoustic Engineer)
Gardiner & Theobald
(Cost Consultant)
Theatre Projects
(Theatre Consultant)
Anne Minors Performance
(Performance and Seating
Consultant)
Area
6600 sq m / 71,000 sq ft
Value
£16 million / EUR 23 million
Programme
1997–2005

Florida Southern College

Client
Florida Southern College
Team
John McAslan + Partners
(Architect)
Lunz Prebor Fowler, Lakeland
(Executive Architect)
Arup USA
(Multi-disciplinary Engineer)
Earl Walls Associates, San Diego
(Laboratory Planning)
Kvaerner Construction, Inc.
(Contractor)
Area
6000 sq m / 65,000 sq ft
Value
$10 million / EUR 11.5 million
Programme
1993–2000

78–80 Derngate

Client
78 Derngate Trust
Team
John McAslan + Partners
(Architect)
Jampel, Davison and Bell
(Structural Engineer)
Rybka Battle
(Services Engineer)
JMP Landscape
(Landscape Architect)
Boyden & Company
(Cost Consultant)
William Anelay
(Contractor)
Area
325 sq m / 3500 sq ft
Value
£2.5 million / EUR 4 million
Programme
1998–2003

De La Warr Pavilion

Client
Rother District Council /
Pavilion Charitable Trust
Team
John McAslan+ Partners
(Architect)
F.J. Samuely & Partners
(Structural Engineer)
Rybka Battle (Services Engineer)
Maynard Mortimer & Gibbons
(Cost Consultant)
Area
4000 sq m / 43,000 sq ft
Value
£8 million / EUR 12 million
Programme
1991–2005

Swiss Cottage Library

Client
London Borough of Camden
Team
John McAslan + Partners
(Architect)
John Wolfenden
(Project Manager)
Whitby Bird & Partners
(Structural Engineer)
Gifford & Partners
(Services Engineer)
E.C. Harris (Cost Consultant)
Sunley Turiff (Contractor)
Area
5000 sq m / 54,000 sq ft
Value
£5 million / EUR 8 million
Programme
1999–2003

Peter Jones Store

Client
John Lewis Partnership
Team
John McAslan + Partners
(Architect)
John Lewis Partnership
Building Group with
Bamber and Reddan
(Executive Architect)
Hurst, Peirce & Malcolm
(Structural Engineer)
Troup Bywaters & Anders
(Services Engineer)
Davis, Langdon & Everest
(Cost Consultant)
FPD Savills (Planning Consultant)
Bovis Lend Lease
(Management Contractor)
Area
30,000 sq m / 323,000 sq ft
Value
£100 million / EUR 148 million
Programme
1997–2004

Max Mara Headquarters

Client
Max Mara Fashion Group
Team
John McAslan + Partners
(Architect)
Arcdesign (Executive Architect)
Intertecno SpA Milan
(Multi-disciplinary Engineer)
Peter Walker & Partners
(Landscape Architect)
Ambiente Europa
(Contractor)
Unieco S.c.r.l.
(Contractor)
Frabboni S.p.A
(Contractor)
Area
45,000 sq m / 485,000 sq ft
Value
£40 million / EUR 59 million
Programme
1996–2004

Yapi Kredi Operations Centre

Client
Yapi Kredi Bank, Turkey
Team
John McAslan + Partners
(Architect)
Arup
(Multi-disciplinary Engineer)
Peter Walker & Partners
(Landscape Architect)
Baytur
(Contractor)
Area
65,000 sq m / 700,000 sq ft
Value
£50 million / EUR 74 million
Programme
1996–1999

Yapi Kredi Headquarters

Client
Yapi Kredi Bank, Turkey
Team
John McAslan + Partners
(Architect)
Arup
(Multi-disciplinary Engineer)
Edward Hutchison
(Landscape Architect)
Area
15,000 sq m / 161,000 sq ft
Value
£12 million / EUR 17 million
Programme
2002–2006

60 Fenchurch Street

Client
Frogmore Estates
Team
John McAslan + Partners
(Architect)
Price & Myers
(Structural Engineer)
Rybka Battle
(Services Engineer)
Maunsell Faber
(Fire Engineer)
Wintech
(Façade Engineer)
Hann Tucker
(Acoustic Engineer)
Denis Wilson Partnership
(Transportation Engineer)
JMP Landscape
(Landscape Architect)
Gardiner & Theobald
(Cost Consultant)
Montagu Evans
(Planning Consultant)
Kier
(Management Contractor)
Area
8000 sq m / 86,000 sq ft
Value
£14.5 million / EUR 21.5 million
Programme
2000–2004

Centre de Solar

Client
Suntrans Real Estate
Development Co. Ltd, Beijing
Team
John McAslan + Partners
(Architect and Masterplanner)
Beijing Institute of Architectural
Design and Research
(Executive Architect)
Parsons Brinckerhoff
(Services Engineer)
Area
70,000 sq m / 753,000 sq ft
Value
n/a
Programme
2003–2006

Benenden Hospital

Client
Benenden Hospital Trust
Team
John McAslan + Partners
(Architect)
Arup
(Multi-disciplinary Engineer)
Faithful & Gould
(Cost Consultant)
Robert Owen Associates
(Medical Specialist)
Hurley Palmer Flatt
(Planning Supervisor)
Wallis Ltd
(Contractor)
Area
1850 sq m / 20,000 sq ft
Value
£2.8 million / EUR 4 million
Programme
1999–2002

Manchester Metropolitan University Law Faculty

Client
Manchester Metropolitan
University
Team
John McAslan + Partners
(Architect)
Buro Happold
(Multi-disciplinary Engineer)
Walfords
(Cost Consultant and Project
Manager)
BCA Project Services
(Planning Supervisor)
Shepherd Construction Ltd
(Contractor)
Area
5500 sq m / 59,000 sq ft
Value
£10 million / EUR 14 million
Programme
2000–2003

University of Southampton Engineering Building

Client
University of Southampton
Team
John McAslan + Partners
(Architect)
Anthony Ward Partnership Ltd
(Structural Engineer)
Parsons Brinckerhoff
(Services Engineer)
JMP Landscape
(Landscape Architect)
James Nisbet & Partners
(Cost Consultant)
Area
7000 sq m / 75,000 sq ft
Value
£10 million / EUR 14 million
Programme
2003–2005

De La Salle School

Client
De La Salle School
Team
John McAslan + Partners
(Architect)
Clancey Consulting
(Structural Engineer)
Buro Happold
(Services Engineer)
AEC
(Acoustic Engineer)
Goth Hibbert
(Cost Consultant)
Nobles Construction Ltd
(Contractor)
Area
750 sq m / 8000 sq ft
Value
£750,000 / EUR 1.2 million
Programme
2002–2004

Sure Start Lavender Nursery

Client
London Borough of Merton
Team
John McAslan + Partners
(Architect)
Arup
(Multi-disciplinary Engineer)
JMP Landscape
(Landscape Architect)
Boyden & Company
(Cost Consultant)
Area
1000 sq m / 10,800 sq ft
Value
£1.4 million / EUR 2.1 million
Programme
2002–2004

King's Cross Station

Client
Network Rail Infrastructure Ltd
Team
John McAslan + Partners
(Architect)
Arup
(Multi-disciplinary Engineer)
JMP Landscape
(Landscape Architect)
Faithful & Gould
(Cost Consultant)
Arup JDC
(Servicing and
Logistics Consultant)
Tweeds Project Services
(Planning Supervisor)
Area
11,700 sq m / 126,000 sq ft
Value
£275 million / EUR 408 million
Programme
1998–2009

Crossrail Paddington Station

Client
Cross London Rail Links
Team
John McAslan + Partners
(Architect)
Connell Mott MacDonald
(Multi-disciplinary Engineer)
JMP Landscape
(Landscape Architect)
Corduroys / Gardiner &
Theobald
(Cost Consultant)
Area
16,000 sq m / 172,000 sq ft
Value
£200 million / EUR 297 million
Programme
2003–2010

Piccadilly Gardens Interchange

Client
Greater Manchester Passenger
Transport Executive
Team
John McAslan + Partners
(Architect)
Arup
(Multi-discipinary Engineer)
JMP Landscape
(Landscape Architect)
Davis, Langdon & Everest
(Cost Consultant)
Area
n/a
Value
£3 million / EUR 5 million
Programme
2003–2005

Kelvin Link Bridge

Client
University of Glasgow
Team
John McAslan + Partners
(Architect)
Anthony Hunt Associates
(Structural Engineer)
Churchman Associates
(Landscape Architect)
Sutton Vane Associates
(Lighting Designer)
Ron Haselden (Artist)
Davis, Langdon & Everest
(Cost Consultant)
Area
n/a
Value
£1 million / EUR 1.5 million
Programme
1999–2005

St George's Island

Client
Dandara Ltd
Team
John McAslan + Partners
(Architect)
Dandara Commercial Ltd
(Structural Engineer)
Hulley & Kirkwood
(Services Engineer)
Arup
(Fire Engineer)
Arup
(Acoustic Engineer)
JMP Landscape
(Landscape Architect)
Dandara Ltd
(Cost Consultant)
McGurk Safety Consultants Ltd
(Planning Supervisor)
Area
20,000 sq m / 215,000 sq ft
Value
£38 million / EUR 56 million
Programme
2003–2007

182–188 Kensington Church Street

Client
Grainger Trust
Team
John McAslan + Partners
(Architect)
Arup
(Multi-disciplinary Engineer)
Davis, Langdon & Everest
(Cost Consultant)
FPD Savills
(Planning Consultant)
Area
3000 sq m / 32,000 sq ft
Value
£3 million / EUR 5 million
Programme
2003–2006

SELECTED PROJECTS

Projects from 1984 to 1995
are by Troughton McAslan.

**Design House
Camden, London**
Design House

1984

**Shepherd's Bush Studios
Hammersmith & Fulham
London**
Michael Peters Group

1985

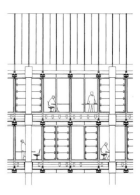

**Allied Breweries Headquarters
Burton upon Trent**
Allied Breweries

**Indira Gandhi National
Centre for Arts
New Delhi, India**
Government of India

1986

**Petershill
City of London**
MEPC

1987

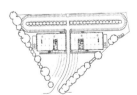

Capability Green
Luton
Lyfgun Properties

Pond Place
Kensington & Chelsea, London
Local London Group

1988

British High Commission
Nairobi, Kenya
British Foreign &
Commonwealth Office

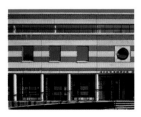

Alexander House
Merton, London
Shilton plc

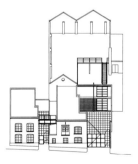

3 St Peter's Street
Islington, London
Derwent Valley Holdings

1989

Lipstick Building
Docklands, London
London Docklands
Development Corporation

Apple Computers Headquarters
Stockley Park
Stockley Park Consortium
& Apple Computers

St Catherine's College
Kobe Institute
Kobe, Japan
Kobe Steel
St Catherine's College

Leeds Corridors Initiative
Leeds
Leeds City Council

Redhill Station
Redhill
British Rail Board

Princes Dock
Liverpool
Liverpool Development Corporation

De La Warr Pavilion
Bexhill-on-Sea
Rother District Council

Tower Place Redevelopment
City of London
Bowring Group

Princes Tower
Rotherhithe, London
Private client

1–3 Colebrooke Place
Islington, London
Derwent Valley Holdings

National Museum of Scotland
Edinburgh
National Museum of Scotland

1 St Peter's Street
Islington, London
Derwent Valley Holdings

1990

1991

Legal Affairs and Judiciary Building
Victoria, Seychelles
Republic of Seychelles

Il Molino
San Gimignano, Italy
Private client

Vocational Training Centre
Acton, London
London Underground Ltd

Bolsover Street
Westminster, London
Great Portland Estates

Hardwick Street
Islington, London
London Merchant Securities

25 The North Colonnade
Canary Wharf, London
Olympia & York Canary Wharf Ltd

Heathrow Terminal 3
Hillingdon, London
British Airports Authority

Hunslet Mills
Leeds
Leeds Development Corporation
English Heritage

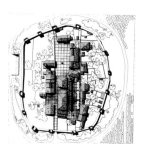

Monteriggioni
Tuscany, Italy
Commune di Monteriggioni

Middlesex House
Camden, London
Derwent Valley Holdings

Rosebery Avenue
Islington, London
London Merchant Securities

London Institute
Southwark, London
London Borough of Southwark

Cincinnati Art Museum
Cincinnati, USA
Cincinnati Art Museum

1992   **1993**

Royal Society of Arts
Westminster, London
Royal Society of Arts

London Bridge Station
Southwark, London
Railtrack Major Projects

Elevated Road and Train System
Bangkok, Thailand
Hopewell Securities

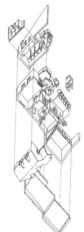

Imperial College Sherfield Building
Westminster, London
Imperial College of Science,
Technology and Medicine

South Bank Centre
Lambeth, London
South Bank Centre

Barbara Hepworth Museum
St Ives
Tate Gallery

Commonwealth Institute
Kensington & Chelsea, London
Commonwealth Institute

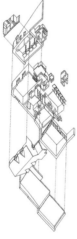

Einstein Tower
Potsdam, Germany
Astrological Institute of Postdam

Peckham Square
Southwark, London
London Borough of Southwark

Crossrail Dean Street Station
Westminster, London
London Underground Ltd

Isokon Flats
Camden, London
London Borough of Camden

1994

1995

Christopher Place
Camden, London
Speech Language and Hearing Centre

Premier House
Westminster, London
Derwent Valley Holdings

Lange Voorhout
The Hague, Netherlands
MAB

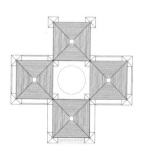

Trenton Bath House
New Jersey, USA
Jewish Community Center

1996

Royal Society of Arts
Great Room
Westminster, London
Royal Society of Arts

Waverley Station
Edinburgh
Scotrail

Hat Factory
Luckenwalde, Germany
Luckenwalde Town Council

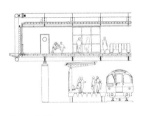

Three Bridges
Crawley, West Sussex
London Transport and
London Underground Ltd

West End Green
Westminster, London
Waterfront Development

New Cross Gate Scheme
Lewisham, London
Thameslink 2000

1997

Imperial College Library
Westminster, London
Imperial College of Science,
Technology and Medicine

School of Oriental and African Studies
Camden, London
School of Oriental and African Studies

Heathrow Express Rail Link
Paddington Station
Westminster, London
Railtrack Major Projects

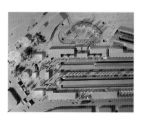

King's Cross Station
Masterplan Feasibility
Camden, London
Network Rail Infrastructure Ltd

Passenger Terminal
Muan Airport, South Korea
Government of South Korea

The Moat School
Hammersmith & Fulham,
London
The Constable Educational Trust

LIFE
Hounslow, London
Argent

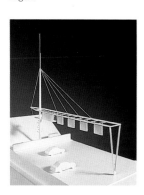

Motorway Gantry System
United Kingdom
Highways Agency

Whitechapel Art Gallery
Tower Hamlets, London
Whitechapel Art Gallery

Hounslow East Station
Hounslow, London
London Underground Ltd

Canning Town Bus Station
Newham, London
London Underground Ltd

Queen Victoria Street
City of London
Salvation Army

Canning Town Station
Newham, London
London Underground Ltd

Imperial College Boat Club
Wandsworth, London
Imperial College of Science,
Technology and Medicine

Thames & Hudson Headquarters
Camden, London
Thames & Hudson

Agora Headquarters
Warsaw, Poland
Agora

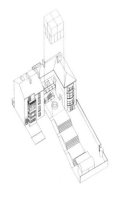

82 Derngate
Northampton
The Derngate Trust

Stratford Station
Accommodation Building
Newham, London
London Underground Ltd

Yapi Kredi Operations Centre
Istanbul, Turkey
Yapi Kredi Bank

1998   **1999**

Sutton Row
Westminster, London
Derwent Valley Holdings

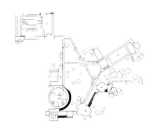

Polk County Science Building
Lakeland, Florida, USA
Florida Southern College

Florida Southern College
Esplanade Canopies
Lakeland, Florida, USA
Florida Southern College

Queen's University
Students' Centre
Belfast
Queen's University

Ferenc Liszt Music Academy
Budapest, Hungary
Ferenc Liszt Music Academy

Southwark Tower
Southwark, London
Private client

BBC White City
Hammersmith & Fulham, London
British Broadcasting Corporation

Queen Victoria Street Visitor Centre
City of London
Salvation Army

Besiktas JK Stadium
Istanbul, Turkey
Besiktas

Royal Academy of Music
Recital Hall
Westminster, London
Royal Academy of Music

2000

2001

Fresh Kills
Staten Island, USA
City of New York,
Department of Planning

Museum of Zoology
Cambridge
University of Cambridge

Trinity College of Music
Greenwich, London
Trinity College of Music

Benenden Hospital
Kent
Benenden Hospital Trust

Palace Gate
Kensington & Chelsea, London
10 Palace Gate

Paddington Central Phase III
Westminster, London
Development Securities Ltd

Stock Exchange Redevelopment
City of London
The Stock Exchange

2002

Peel Park
Blackpool
Land Securities Trillium

Swiss Cottage Library
Camden, London
London Borough of Camden

78–80 Derngate
Northampton
The Derngate Trust

Leicester Square
Westminster, London
Prudential Property Management

High Line
New York, USA
Friends of The High Line

2003

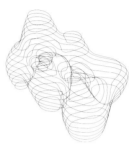

Park Street
Southwark, London
Chelsfield plc

Manchester Metropolitan University
Law Faculty
Manchester
Manchester Metropolitan University

Borusan Holdings Headquarters
Istanbul, Turkey
Borusan Holdings

Middlesbrough Town Hall
Middlesbrough
Middlesbrough Borough Council

Sure Start Lavender Nursery
Mitcham, London
London Borough of Merton

3 Hardman Square
Manchester
Allied London Properties

Piccadilly Gardens Interchange
Manchester
Greater Manchester Passenger
Transport Executive

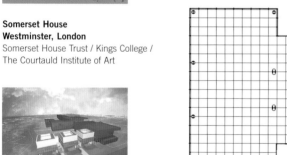

Peter Jones Store
Kensington & Chelsea, London
John Lewis Partnership

Max Mara Headquarters
Reggio Emilia, Italy
Max Mara Fashion Group

Dorset Square
Westminster, London
London Merchant Securities

Somerset House
Westminster, London
Somerset House Trust / Kings College /
The Courtauld Institute of Art

60 Fenchurch Street
City of London
Frogmore Estates

Roundhouse
Camden, London
Norman Trust

De La Salle School
Centre for the Performing Arts
St Helens
De La Salle School

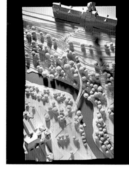

Cyril House
Camden, London
Private client

Kelvin Link Bridge
Glasgow
Glasgow University

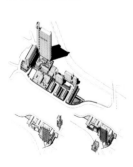

Trellick Tower
Kensington & Chelsea, London
Royal Borough of Kensington and Chelsea

School of Oriental and African Studies
East Wing Building
Camden, London
School of Oriental and African Studies

Southampton University
Engineering Building
Southampton
University of Southampton

De La Warr Pavilion
Bexhill-on-Sea
Rother District Council
Pavilion Charitable Trust

2004

2005

Centre de Solar
Beijing, China
Suntrans Real Estate
Development Co. Ltd

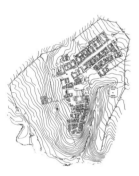

Volubilis Site Museum
Moulay Idriss, Morocco
Royaume du Maroc
Ministère des Affaires Culturelles

Ifrane Cultural Centre
Ifrane, Morocco
Al Akhawayn University

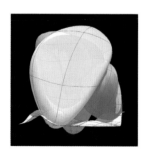

182–188 Kensington Church Street
Kensington & Chelsea, London
Grainger Trust

Seager
Lewisham, London
Brookmill Estates

Gateway Building
Lakeland, Florida, USA
Florida Southern College

Oval Road
Camden, London
Railway Pension Nominees Ltd

Yapi Kredi Headquarters
Istanbul, Turkey
Yapi Kredi Bank

Baron's Keep
Hammersmith & Fulham, London
Baron's Keep

Golden Square
Westminster, London
Hague Securities

Silver City
Westminster, London
BP Management Ltd

Lodge Road
Westminster, London
EDF Energy Property

St George's Island
Manchester
Dandara Ltd

Sugar Warehouse
Greenock
The Prince of Wales's
Phoenix Trust

2008

Royal Welsh College of Music and Drama
Cardiff
Royal Welsh College of Music and Drama

King's Cross Station
Camden, London
Network Rail Infrastructure Ltd

2009

Crossrail Paddington Station
Westminster, London
Cross London Rail Links

2010

Ranchi
Jharkhand, India
Government of Jharkhand

2011

West London Development
Acton, London
Sellar Property Group

STUDIO MEMBERS

2004 onwards

Temoor Ahmad
Tennill Alexander
Julian Anderson
Hiro Aso
Phillip Blackshaw
Adam Brown
Matthew Burl
Claire Calderbank
Martin Canaway
Christian Coop
Erica Cotton
Chris Crombie
Rachel Cruise
Ben Davidson
Alex de Blonay
Zoë Donoff
Yvonne Douglas
Richard Ellis
Umberto Emoli
Devan Foster
Dan Gibson
Trevore Grams
Nick Hacking
Richard Haddock
Eric Hallquist
Quintin Hinxman
Georgina Hock
Thomas Karcher
Russell Kenny
Tina Komninou
Hannah Lawson
Kim Lenaghan
John McAslan
Greg McLean
Katherina Machule
Natasha Martin
Joe Morgan

Emma Neville
Jo Newman
Dean Nicholas
Karl Normanton
Don Orike
Monika Paarmann
Sonia Pabla
Fanos Panayides
Jacek Pazdzior
Aidan Potter
Andrew Pryke
Frederik Rissom
Claire Sa
Jonathan Shaw
Tony Skipper
Jim Sloane
Chris Smiles
Dominique Smith
Murray Smith
Andy Snow
Noelie Srivastava
Mieke Tanghe
Andrew Thornhill
Alasdair Travers
Juliette Truman
Nick Vaughan
Kate Walsh
Barbara Witt
Oliver Wong
Roger Wu

1984–2003

Soji Abass
Joanna Ako
Charlotte Anderson
Stephen Archer
Juliette Aston
Bob Atwal
Mohammed Azhar
Nick Bailey
Peter Beard
Christina Belton
Alison Bick
Janet Brown
Catriona Burns
James Burrell
Karly Cameron
Martin Campbell
Michael Chadwick
Nini Cheng
Neil Clark
Jason Cornish
Robin Cross
Paul Davey
Sharon Davis
Leslie Day
Bobby Desai
Madelaine Deschamps
Eamon Doyle
Ashley Dunn
Michael Durran
Christopher Egret
Nick Eldridge
Stuart Elgie
Fidan Erdal
Olivia Frazer
Adrian Friend
Yasser el Gabry
Jose Aguilar Garcia
Colin Glover
Hans Grabowski
Rui Grazina
Joanna Greenoak
Simon Grimby
Thomas Grotzeck
Andrew Hapgood
Martin Harris
Kerstin Hartmann
Alison Henry
Jonathan Hill
Marianne Hilpert
Annabel Hodgson
Marysia Holland
Martin Hopp
Simon Hunt
Ken Hutt

Dinka Izetbegovic
Jean-Paul Jaccaud
Sarah Jackson
Nicola James
Glenn Jeffrey
Lucy Jenkins
Vanessa Johnson
Jeremy King
Yoon King Chong
Michael Kininmonth
Dean Kirkwood
Birgit Klauk
Michelle Krausz
Merethe Kristensen
Isabel Kung
Sadie LaDuc
James Lambert
Scott Lawrie
Kuan Leng
Daniel Lewandowski
Kit Lewis
Kevin Lloyd
Vanessa Locket
James Macauley
Ian McChesney
Malcolm McGregor
Colin Mackenzie
Jan Mackie
Jennifer Mallard
Martin Markcrow
Nebojsa Marojevic
Catherine Martin
Christopher Mascall
Bianca Mathews
Roger Meadows
David Medas
Cecile Menon
Nick Midgeley
Ruth Miller
Sarah Mitchell
Patricia Miyamoto
Ali Mohajery
Kwamina Monney
Peter Morris
Gary Mountford
Michelle Mumby
Matthew Murfett
Olu Olutayo
Ezekiel Osho
Jonathan Parr
James Parritt
Rosemary Pattison
Debbie Paul
Nick Pawlik
Sarah-Jane Pearce
Lynton Pepper
Michael Pepper
Pedro Pereira

Chris Perry
Jan-Marc Petroschka
Michael Pike
Stephen Pimbley
Suzie Pote
Matthew Priestman
Judith Quartson
James Reed
Gemma Robinson
Grant Robinson
Raj Rooprai
Marcos Rosello
Michele Le Roux
Ryan von Ruben
Stella Sargeson
Jamie Shorton
Zoka Skorup
Judy Slater
Rachel Smart
Piers Smerin
Colin Smith
Gavin Smith
Stephanie Smith
Ed Soden
Elaine Stevenson
Magnus Strom
Paul Summerlin
Paul Swann
Maureen Tadman
Yan Taylor
Ian Troake
Jamie Troughton
Jo Veasey
Paul Voysey
Anne Wagner
Tracie Walter
Martin Weaver
Cecily Weld
Pat West
Andrew Weston
David Whitehead
Matt Williams
Mark Wilson
Jane Witz
Marek Wojciechowski

Clockwise from right:
1996, 1990, 1985, 1998, 2000

PUBLICATIONS

Acton Vocational Training Centre
1990, September, *FP Fusion Planning*
(Japan)

Alexander House
1989, 5 April, *The Architects' Journal*

Apple Computers Headquarters
1988, May, *Business*
1989, April, *Architecture Intérieure
Crée* (France)
1989, April, *Blueprint*
1989, April, *Techniques et
Architecture* (France)
1989, May, *The Architectural Review*
1989, 4 August, *Building*
1989, October, *L'Arca* (Italy)
1989, 25 October, *The Sunday Telegraph*
1989, 27 October, *Building Design*
1989, December, *Progressive
Architecture* (USA)
1990, March, *AJ Focus*
1990, May, *Baumeister* (Germany)
1990, 13 June, *Immeubles de
Bureaux* (France)
1991, October, *Ediciones Atrium
SA* (Spain)

Benenden Hospital
2003, 10 April, *The Architects' Journal*
2003, July, *Abitare* (Italy)
2003, 11 September, *New Civil Engineer*
2003 *New Architecture in Britain*
(London: Merrell)

Borusan Holdings Headquarters
2002, 5 September, *The Architects' Journal*

British High Commission, Nairobi
1989, 8 December, *Building Design*

Canning Town and Stratford Stations
1992, 21 October, *The Architects' Journal*
1992, 23 October, *Building Design*
1997, 14 February, *Building*
1997, October, *Jubilee Journal*
1999, May, *The Architectural Review*
1999, 2 May, *Financial Times*
2000, February, *Architecture Today*
2000, 18 February, *Building*
2000, March, *Arquitectura Viva* (Spain)
2000, May, *Casabella* (Italy)
2000, June, *Deutsche Bauzeitung*
(Germany)
2000, October, *Concrete*
2001, July, *Architecture Today*

Capability Green
1989, 27 October, *Building Design*

Centre de Solar
2003, 4 July, *Building Design*
2003, 8 August, *Building Design*

Christopher Place
1994, 8 April, *Building Design*
1995, May, *RIBA Journal*
1995, November, *RIBA Journal*
1996, March, *The Arup Journal*
1996, November, *Architectural
Record* (USA)
1998, March, *Junior*

1–3 Colebrooke Place
1991, July, *Ediciones Atrium SA* (Spain)

Commonwealth Institute
1990, 4 October, *Building Design*

Crossrail Dean Street Station
1991, 11 November, *The Scotsman*
1993, 22 October, *Building Design*

De La Salle School
2002, 5 December, *The Architects' Journal*
2002, 6 December, *Building*
2002, 6 December, *Building Design*
2003, January, *FX*

De La Warr Pavilion
1991, 23 November, *The Guardian*
1991, 11 December, *The Independent*
1992, 14 February, *Building*
1992, May, *Baumeister* (Germany)
1992, 30 July, *Country Life*
1992, 6 August, *New Builder*
1992, December, *Building*
1993, 28 November, *The Sunday Times*
1994, 16 February, *The Architects' Journal*
1994, March, *European Architectural
Heritage*
1995, February, *Detail* (Germany)
1995, March, *Tasarim* (Turkey)
1995, April, *Architektur* (Austria)
1995, November, *Conservation Bulletin*
1996, 31 March, *Style*
1996, 14 September, *Weekend Telegraph*
1996, 28 September, *Financial Times*
1998, March, *Modern Movement Heritage*
1999, February, *Private Eye*
2000, 14 February, *The Daily Telegraph*
2000, 18 February, *Building Design*
2000, March, *Contemporary Staircases*
2000, 27 March, *The Guardian*
2000, 31 July, *The Independent*
2000, 9 September, *The Times*
2000, 19 September, *The Times*
2002, 16 April, *The Guardian*
2002, 11 July, *The Architects' Journal*
2002, 13 July, *The Independent Magazine*
2002, 20 August, *The Daily Telegraph*
2003, February, *Building for Leisure*
2003, July, *Shifting Sands: Design and the
Changing Image of English Seaside Towns*
(London: English Heritage / CABE)

78–80 Derngate
1995, 10 February, *Building Design*
1999, 22 October, *Building*
2001, 21 September, *The Guardian*
2002, 17 May, *Building Design*
2003, December, *AJ Focus*
2003, 13 December, *The Herald Magazine*
2004, 12 February, *The Architects' Journal*
2004, 14 February, *The Independent
Magazine*

Design House
1984, 25 January, *The Architects' Journal*
1984, September, *Interior Design*

Einstein Tower
1993, 3 November, *The Architects' Journal*
1993, 5 November, *Building Design*
1993, 12 November, *New Builder*
1994, November, *BCB Journal*

60 Fenchurch Street
2001, 26 May, *Estates Gazette*
2001, 22 June, *Building*
2002, March, *JMP Journal*
2003, September, *Landlines*

Florida Southern College
1993, August, *RIBA Journal*
1994, 27 February, *The Sunday Telegraph*
1995, January, *The Arup Journal*
1995, 3 March, *Building Design*
1995, September, *Building Renovation*
1995, September, *Progressive Architecture*
  (USA)
1995, 6 October, *Building Design*
1997, 8 May, *The Architects' Journal*
1999, December, *Laboratory*
1999, December, *RIBA Journal*
2001, 15 November, *The Architects'*
  Journal
2001, 22 November, *The Architects'*
  Journal

Fresh Kills
2001, 12 October, *Building*
2001, December, *Landlines*
2001, 9 December, *New York Times* (USA)
2002, 11 January, *Building Design*
2002, February, *The Municipal Art*
  Society Newsletter (USA)
2002, June, *Competitions* (USA)
2002, June, *Landscape Architecture*
2002, 27 June, *New Civil Engineer*
2002, September, *World Architecture*
2002, 20 September, *Building*
2002, November, *Landlines*
2002, November, *Praxis* (USA)
2002, December, *JMP Journal*

3 Hardman Square
2002, 29 November, *Property Week*
2003, 16 January, *The Architects' Journal*
2003, 17 January, *Building*
2003, 17 January, *Building Design*
2003, February, *Update Allied*

Hardwick Street
1992, May, *Architecture Today*
1993, October, *AJ Focus*
1993, November, *AJ Focus*

Hat Factory
1998, March, *Ruins of Modernity*
  (London: Architectural Association)

Hounslow East Station
1997, 8 May, *The Architects' Journal*

Il Molino
1993, 28 January, *Country Life*
1993, November, *Abitare* (Italy)
1996, August, *Casa da Abitare* (Italy)

Imperial College Library
1995, 25 June, *Building Design*
1997, February, *RIBA Journal*
1998, 15 January, *The Architects' Journal*
1998, March, *AJ Focus*
1998, October, *Abitare* (Italy)

Indira Gandhi National Centre for Arts
1987, 13 February, *Building Design*

Isokon Flats
1995, 3 February, *Building Design*
1995, 7 May, *The Sunday Telegraph*
1997, November, *Interiors for Architects*
  & Designers
1998, 8 October, *The Architects' Journal*
1999, 15 March, *The Independent*

Kelvin Link Bridge
1999, May, *L'Arca* (Italy)
1999, 26 November, *The Herald*
1999, 3 December, *The Architects' Journal*
1999, 3 December, *Building Design*
1999, 3 December, *Building*
2000, 5 June, *University Avenue*
2000, 3 November, *Building Design*
2001, 3 May, *The Architects' Journal*
2001, July, *JMP Journal*
2003, 11 September, *The Herald*

King's Cross Station
1999, 3 December, *Building*
2001, 23 November, *Property Week*
2003, 12 January, *The Sunday Times*

Lipstick Building
1990, 3 August, *The Architects' Journal*
1994, August, *RIBA Journal*

Manchester Metropolitan University Law Faculty
2001, 10 May, *The Architects' Journal*
2001, 7 July, *The Architects' Journal*
2001, 12 July, *The Architects' Journal*
2001, 13 July, *Building Design*
2003, June, *Prospect NW*
2003, 17 September, *City Life*

Max Mara Headquarters
2001, March, *JMP Journal*

Middlesex House
1993, November, *The Architectural*
  Review

Monteriggioni
1993, 6 June, *Financial Times*

Motorway Gantry System
1998, 1 May, *The Architects' Journal*
1998, 12 June, *Building Design*

25 The North Colonnade
1989, 31 March, *Building Design*
1989, 21 April, *Building*
1989, 21 April, *Building Design*
1989, 1 May, *Blueprint*
1989, 26 November, *New York Times*
1989, 15 December, *Building Design*
1991, January, *29th Report, Royal Fine*
  Art Commission
1991, 30 August, *Evening Standard*
1991, 4 October, *Building*
1992, 28 January, *The Times*
1992, 1 April, *The Independent*
1994, 15 September, *Property Week*
1998, 19 November, *The Wharf*

Peckham Square
1994, December, *RIBA Journal*

Peter Jones Store
1998, 5 June, *Building Design*
1999, 5 March, *Building*
1999, 27 March, *Evening Standard*
2001, 6 April, *Building*
2001, 14 July, *The Gazette*
2001, *New London Architecture*
  (London: Merrell)

Pond Place
1988, November, *RIBA Journal*

Princes Tower

1986, 16 July, *The Architects' Journal*
1986, 28 July, *The Guardian*
1986, 4 August, *The Daily Telegraph*
1987, February, *Architectural Record* (USA)
1987, July, *L'Arca* (Italy)
1988, 23 April, *The Daily Telegraph*
1988, 29 April, *The Independent*
1990, 22 February, *Country Life*
1990, March, *BBC Design 1990 Catalogue*
1991, 30 August, *Evening Standard*
1991, September, *aw architektur + wettbewerbe* (Germany)

Queen Victoria Street Visitor Centre

1998, 7 August, *The Times*
1999, 30 July, *Building*
2001, 2 February, *Building*
2001, *New London Architecture* (London: Merrell)

Redhill Station

1989, January, *L'Arca* (Italy)
1989, 6 October, *Building*
1989, 10 November, *Building Design*
1991, 13 March, *The Architects' Journal*
1991, April, *AJ Focus*
1991, 3 May, *The Architects' Journal*
1991, October, *Baumeister* (Germany)
1991, November, *a+t* (Spain)
1992, 25 September, *Building Design*
1992, December, *Abitare* (Italy)
1995, June, *Tasarim* (Turkey)
2001, 28 February, *Country Life*

Rosebery Avenue

1988, 2 December, *Building Design*
1989, May, *The Architectural Review*
1992, 8 January, *Estates Gazette*
1992, 7 February, *Building Design*
1992, May, *Architecture Today*
1993, October, *AJ Focus*
1993, November, *AJ Focus*

Roundhouse

1997, 8 May, *The Architects' Journal*
1997, 5 December, *Building Design*
1998, 24 January, *Evening Standard*
1998, 8 February, *The Sunday Telegraph*
1998, 18 May, *The Times*
1998, 24 November, *Evening Standard*
1998, 25 November, *Financial Times*
1998, 25 November, *The Independent*
1998, 25 November, *The Times*
1998, 26 November, *The Architects' Journal*
1999, 8 March, *The Times*
2001, 19 March, *The Daily Telegraph*
2001, 3 October, *Evening Standard*
2001, *New London Architecture* (London: Merrell)
2002, 12 September, *The Architects' Journal*
2002, 13 September, *Building*
2002, 13 September, *Property Week*
2002, 14 September, *Estates Gazette*
2002, October November *Civic & Public Buildings Specifier*
2003, 30 January, *The Architects' Journal*
2003, September, *AXIS* (Japan)

Royal Academy of Music

1999, 7 May, *The Architects' Journal*
2001, January, *RAM Newsletter*
2001, 23 February, *Building*
2001, 7 December, *Building Design*
2001, *New London Architecture* (London: Merrell)
2002, 13 June, *The Architects' Journal*
2002, 26 September, *New Civil Engineer*
2002, October, *Concrete*
2003, 2 April, *Architecture Week*

Royal Society of Arts

1996, December, *RSA Journal*
1997, February, *The Architectural Review*

Royal Welsh College of Music & Drama

2002, November, *Touchstone*
2002, 5 December, *The Architects' Journal*

St Catherine's College Institute

1989, 8 November, *Building Design*
1990, 2 November, *Building Design*
1990, 7 November, *The Architects' Journal*
1990, 11 November, *The Sunday Times*
1991, 25 September, *The Times*
1991, 29 September, *The Sunday Times*
1991, November, *The Architectural Review*
1991, November, *Blueprint*
1991, November, *Kenchiku Bunka* (Japan)
1991, 8 November, *Building Design*
1991, 13 November, *The Independent*
1991, 18 November, *The Times*
1992, 22 June, *Nikkei Architecture* (Japan)
1992, October, *L'Arca* (Italy)
1992, December, *Okura Lantern* (Japan)
1993, January, *Best of British Architecture*
1993, March, *Industrial Britain*
1993, 10 March, *Journal of Architecture* (Japan)
1994, 21 January, *Building Design*
1994, August, *President's Choice: An Exhibition of Architecture at the Royal West of England Academy*
1994, October, *L'Industria Italiana del Cemento* (Italy)

1–3 St Peter's Street

1988, 9 September, *Building*
1988, 10 November, *The Architects' Journal*
1989, 6 April, *Country Life*
1990, December, *Abitare* (Italy)

School of Oriental and African Studies

1998, August, *Hiroba* (Japan)
1999, 8 October, *Building Design*
1999, 9 October, *Building*

Seager

2001, 19 April, *The Architects' Journal*
2001, 20 April, *Building*
2001, 20 April, *Building Design*
2001, 7 July, *Estates Gazette*
2001, 20 October, *Estates Gazette*
2002, 11 January, *Building*
2002, 11 January, *Property Week*
2002, 12 January, *Estates Gazette*
2002, 8 March, *Property Week*
2002, 19 April, *The Architects' Journal*
2002, 19 April, *Building*
2002, 28 June, *Property Week*

Shepherd's Bush Studios
1986, March, *The Architectural Review*
1986, April, *Architecture Intérieure Crée*
    (France)
1986, September, *Interior Design*

South Bank Centre
1994, March, *Academy Editions*
1994, 15 July, *Building Design*
1994, 23 September, *Building Design*

**Southampton University Engineering
Building**
2003, 20 June, *Building Design*

Sugar Warehouse
2003, 14 February, Building Design

Sure Start Lavender Nursery
2003, 27 March, *The Architects' Journal*
2003, 28 March, *Building Design*

Swiss Cottage Library
2001, 9 March, *Building Design*
2003, August, *RIBA Journal*
2004, July, *RIBA Journal*

Thames & Hudson Headquarters
1999, 23 April, *Building*

Trellick Tower
2002, 21 November, *The Architects'
    Journal*
2002, 22 November, *Building Design*
2003, January, *Il Giornale Dell'Inglese
    Postbellica* (Italy)
2003, 26 January, *The Sunday Times*

Trinity College of Music
1999, September, *Trinity Magazine*
2001, 26 April, *Building*
2001, 5 November, *The Guardian*
2002, 10 October, *The Architects' Journal*
2003, *New Architecture in Britain*
    (London: Merrell)

Volubilis Site Museum
2001, 25 January, *The Architects' Journal*
2001, 31 January, *Evening Standard*
2001, 11 June, *The Daily Mail*
2001, 11 June, *Evening Standard*
2001, 11 June, *The Guardian*
2001, 11 June, *The Times*
2001, 15 June, *Evening Standard*
2001, 29 June, *The Times*
2001, July, *The Architectural Review*
2001, 20 July, *The Times*
2001, September, *The Architectural
    Review*

Waverley Station
1990, 23 February, *Building Design*
1990, 5 March, *The Scotsman*
1990, 12 August, *The Sunday Times*
1990, 29 August, *The Architects' Journal*
1990, December, *aw architektur +
    wettbewerbe* (Germany)
1991, 11 November, *The Scotsman*
1991, 14 November, *The Scotsman*
1992, 10 May, *Sunday Mail*
1992, 11 May, *The Scotsman*
1995, 4 January, *The Times*

Yapi Kredi Operations Centre
1996, 5 December, T*he Architects' Journal*
1996, 6 December, *Building Design*
1997, 7 November, *Building Design*
1997, 13 November, *The Architects'
    Journal*
1998, January, *The Arup Journal*
1998, 16 January, *Building*
1998, 13 February, *Building Design*
1998, March, *The Architectural Review*
1998, May, *YAPI* (Turkey)
1999, March, *Architectural Record* (USA)
2002, November, *L'Industria Italiana
    del Cemento* (Italy)
2003, April, *Staircases – Construction
    & Design*
2003, September, *Umran Magazine* (Saudi
    Arabia)

Practice Profiles / Monographs
1986, 28 July, *Financial Times*
1986, October, *Blueprint*
1988, March, *40 Under Forty*
1988, June, *Architektura* (Poland)
1989, 28 June, *Latter-Day Modernism*
1990, April, *Progressive Architecture*
    (USA)
1990, 15 June, *Process Architecture*
1990, June, *Blueprint*
1991, February, *L'Architecture
    d'Aujourd'hui* (France)
1991, February, *Country Life*
1991, September, *FP Fusion
    Planning* (Japan)
1991, November, *ICON Design +
    Architecture* (Japan)
1992, March, *Baumeister* (Germany)
1992, 8 August, *Estates Gazette*
1993, July, *World Architecture*
1993, 19 November, *Building Design*
1993, 28 November, *The Sunday Times*
1995, June, *Tasarim* (Turkey)
1995, September, *Progressive
    Architecture* (USA)
1996, 6 December, *Building*
1997, 7 Febuary, *Building Design*
1998, 15 January, *The Architects' Journal*
1998, 16 January, *Building*
1998, February, *World Architecture*
1998, December, *Ottagono* (Italy)
1999, 10 June, *The Architects' Journal*
2000, March, *Building*
2000, *John McAslan* (London: Thames
    & Hudson)
2001, 22 March, *The Architects' Journal*
2001, 24 May, *Country Life*
2001, 24 October, *London Now*
2002, 21 March, *The Architects' Journal*
2002, May, *The Architectural Review*
2002, 3 May, *Building*
2002, September, *D line*
2002, September, *FX*
2002, 12 September, *The Budapest Sun*
    (Hungary)
2003, January, *World Architecture –
    Top 300*
2003, February, *Octogon Architecture
    & Design*
2003, May, *Tasarim* (Turkey)
2003, 20 June, *Building*
2003, December, *AJ Focus*
2003, December, *Competitions* (USA)

INDEX

CREDITS

First published by Merrell Publishers Limited

Head office
42 Southwark Street
London SE1 1UN

New York office
49 West 24th Street
New York, NY 10010

www.merrellpublishers.com

Publisher: Hugh Merrell
Editorial Director: Julian Honer
US Director: Joan Brookbank
Sales and Marketing Director: Emilie Amos
Sales and Marketing Executive: Emily Sanders
Managing Editor: Anthea Snow
Editor: Sam Wythe
Design Manager: Nicola Bailey
Production Manager: Michelle Draycott
Design and Production Assistant: Matt Packer

British Library Cataloguing-in-Publication Data:
Powell, Ken, 1947–
    Culture of building : the architecture of John McAslan & Partners
    1.John McAslan & Partners 2.Architecture, Modern – 20th
    century 3.Architecture – Great Britain – 20th century
    4.Architecture, Modern – 21st century 5.Architecture –
    Great Britain – 21st century
    I.Title
    720.9'22

ISBN 1 85894 250 0

Produced by Merrell Publishers
Designed by Thomas Manss & Company
Edited by Murray Smith
Copy-edited by Christine Davis
Indexed by Vicki Robinson

Printed and bound in China

Page 2: Imperial College Library, Westminster, London
Page 32: Royal Academy of Music, Regent's Park, London (see pages 44–53)
Page 58: Roundhouse, Camden, London (see pages 64–69)
Page 70: Swiss Cottage Library, London (see pages 98–103)
Page 114: Max Mara Headquarters, Reggio Emilia, Italy (see pages 116–23)
Page 152: Manchester Metropolitan University Law Faculty (see pages 162–69)
Page 182: Piccadilly Gardens Interchange, Manchester (see pages 198–201)

John McAslan+Partners is one of Britain's most respected and dynamic architectural practices, with projects in the United Kingdom, Europe, North Africa, Asia and the United States. Culture of Building provides a fully up-to-date account of the work of this vibrant studio. Combining detailed project descriptions with plans, drawings and recent photography, this book surveys a wide range of recent and ongoing work – from the Volubilis Visitor Centre and Museum in Morocco and the remodelling of Frank Lloyd Wright's Florida Southern College campus to a major new office complex for Max Mara in Italy and high-profile infrastructure proposals such as the redevelopment of King's Cross Station, London. The book concludes with an illustrated list of key works dating from the studio's inception to the present day, and a selected bibliography of articles and reviews.

Written by Kenneth Powell and with a foreword by Peter Davey, both renowned architecture critics, Culture of Building examines the development and philosophy of the practice, and reveals the way in which John McAslan+Partners' vision of history has informed a highly innovative approach to new design. The result is a celebration of a studio that has made a unique contribution to the architectural scene worldwide.

Kenneth Powell is an architecture critic, journalist and writer. He was architecture correspondent for *The Daily Telegraph* and has published widely, including the books *New London Architecture* and *New Architecture in Britain*, both published by Merrell. He was elected Honorary Fellow of the RIBA in 2000.

Peter Davey is editor of *The Architectural Review*, one of the world's leading architectural journals. He is a qualified architect, and former vice-president of the RIBA.

240 pages, 214 colour and 118 black-and-white illustrations, 110 line drawings

ISBN 1 85894 250-0

90000

9 781858 942506

MERRELL
LONDON · NEW YORK